THE LIVES OF THE SAINTS

SEBASTIAN BARRY

THE LIVES OF THE SAINTS
The Laureate Lectures

faber

First published in 2022
by Faber & Faber Limited
Bloomsbury House
74–77 Great Russell Street
London WC1B 3DA

Typeset by Faber & Faber Limited
Printed and bound by CPI Group (UK) Ltd, Croydon, CRO 4YY

An excerpt from Michael Hartnett's 'Death of an Irishwoman' from
Collected Poems (2001) on p. 31 is reprinted by kind permission of the
Estate of Michael Hartnett and The Gallery Press
www.gallerypress.com

An excerpt from Patrick Kavanagh's 'Shancoduff' from *Collected
Poems* (1964) on p. 23 is reprinted by kind permission of the Estate of
Patrick and Katherine Kavanagh

An excerpt from Thomas Kinsella's 'Mirror in February' from
Collected Poems (2002) on p. 25 is reprinted by kind permission of
Carcanet Press, Manchester, UK

A CIP record for this book
is available from the British Library

ISBN 978-0-571-37202-7

The Laureate for Irish Fiction is an initiative of
The Irish Arts Council/An Chomhairle Ealaíon

2 4 6 8 10 9 7 5 3 1

To Sarah Bannan and Marcella Bannon

CONTENTS

Introduction   1

1   The Lives of the Saints   7
2   Still Life, with Donal   41
3   The Fog of Family   83

Acknowledgements   120

INTRODUCTION

The first of these Laureate Lectures (I might be inclined to put the word in inverted commas, for the sake of honesty) was delivered in the Gate Theatre in 2018, a building adjoined to the Rotunda maternity hospital next door, where no doubt other more important deliveries were taking place. Both buildings are of great importance to me. In the early seventies a lovely friend of mine, having gone into the country to hide out while pregnant, for fear of her father finding out, was now having her baby secretly in the Rotunda. She rang me up from the hospital because she said all the other mothers had husbands or boyfriends, and would I mind coming in and pretending to be the father of her baby. In I went, strangely moved even in that emergency. There was an atmosphere of soldierly courage in that room of about eight women, and great badinage. On the second visit, a poem of mine had just been published in *Hibernia*, and as I entered one of the other young mothers stood up precariously on her bed, and read out the poem with beautiful exuberance. It was like a secret thank you for our deception. My friend and I even named the baby together.

In 1995 my play *The Steward of Christendom* was put on at the Gate, as part of a tour by Out of Joint, the great English theatre company. It's a play that is very much about fathering, it seems to me now, and I wrote it just after the birth of our twins, Merlin and Coral, in 1992, not as it happened in the Rotunda, but Mount Carmel, over in South Dublin. It was about sixteen years after that first experience of 'being a father' – if only in an acting role. In 1998, the Gate was home to *Our Lady of Sligo*, literally a sort of mother/Madonna play.

All these matters were swirling about in my head as I waited backstage before going out to deliver the lecture, not to mention that my own mother had played the Gate stage many times.

I don't know what I expected. Maybe a polite hearing, something like that. My lovely friend Philip Casey the poet had recently died, and the lecture is partly about him, but also about other writers who for their own mys-terious reasons had helped me along as a young writer, and even not so young. I was about to talk about Leland Bardwell, Val Mulkerns and others, and what didn't occur to me was that many people who had known these people, loved them, would be in the audience, including Philip's brother. Perhaps Ireland is still so small that that was inevitable. But it lent a generous energy and magic to me, in the giving of the lecture. The heart and soul of the audience was offered to me as a gift, and 'something happened', as actors sometimes say when they come off stage. Something happened, out there in the light alone, and even more surprising, overwhelming, was the standing ovation at the end. I had written about sixteen plays over the years and I had been so happy when an audience rose to the actors, but I had never experienced the strange gale of feeling which that now gave this solitary creature, who had stood on stage an hour, and delivered a mere lecture in great ignorance, with only a borrowed tincture of courage, possibly, from those Rotunda mothers of long ago.

The second lecture was also given in the Gate, and also seemed very close to home. The publicist for the laureateship, calm and kindly Cormac Kinsella, had reminded me that 2019 would mark the twentieth anniversary of the death of Donal McCann, the 'star' (Donal himself hated the word) of *The Steward of Christendom*. Might it be timely to write a lecture about my experiences with him? It was something I had been avoiding doing, talking about Donal that is, ever since he had died. *The Steward of Christendom*, first put on three years after the birth of the twins, had in truth given my wife Ali and myself more than a signal life experience. I had known Donal in the Abbey since I was a child, and took his commitment to doing a difficult and untried play as very much a sacred matter, very much so. Which is what the lecture tried to get at. But the production also effected the extraordinary magic of bringing enough money to buy a modest house, and created something that was very like an actual income (quite a foreign experience up to that point). It was in any event an intensely familial and personal matter, and when Donal died of cancer in 1999, I was foolish and vulnerable enough to some degree almost to go off into the underworld with him. So it was something I had learned to avoid talking about, even thinking about. Nevertheless, Cormac's seemed like a real inspiration and I undertook to follow his suggestion. I expected so to write about his actual tragic death, and the crushing reaction I had had to it. I wrote the lecture in London in 2019, but in the upshot I never touched on any of that. Instead I wrote about Donal fully alive, triumphant in an impossible Irish play, and the huge sense of friendship and devotion he engendered through the whole enterprise. Which is why I called the lecture 'Still Life, with Donal', because although it was about something fixed and as it were quite still in the past, windless, motionless, yet it was about life, and his nuclear force and consummate elan. Everything that happens in the theatre goes by, and is ultimately and inescapably forgotten, as the generations pass, but my job was to try and fix Donal's work in some sort of loving amber, not a hugely useful thing to do maybe, but as a tribute to what I can only call his timeless genius.

So I delivered that lecture not six feet from where Donal McCann, as the Steward, lay in his humble bed of disarray, where Max Stafford-Clark's perfect production had placed him. I sensed him throughout, just out of my sight, stage right, and feared to hear his famous growl of disapproval. But again, I was speaking to an audience replete with people who had known him, loved him, and even feared him. This was again a unique and unmatchable experience, and I would have to look back at the little film of the event to see if there was another standing ovation at the end. Donal's fierce, loving, exacting silence was reward enough.

Ah, my theatrical career! Then it was over, because of

the sudden pandemic, which has ended so many things, and unexpectedly, started an entirely different way of life for so many. The laureateship had to be hauled up onto platforms online, including the third Laureate Lecture. But that very act of hauling, engineered by the sheer logistical and imaginative brilliance of Marcella Bannon, the facilitator of the laureateship, and Sarah Bannan, the great Head of Literature at the Arts Council, has brought new things, new strategies, and I can regard that in a way as our small victory against the wretched virus, just as that young woman rising on her bed to deliver my poem seemed like a mysterious victory. The third lecture, as I write this, will be given online at the Dublin International Literature Festival in May 2021. I hope it went well! I won't be there, as it were, but my heart will be there, and my soul will be there, and my gratitude for this whole life-giving adventure of the Laureate Lectures.

Moyne, February 2021

THE LIVES OF THE SAINTS

First Laureate Lecture

Given at the Gate Theatre, Dublin
9 September 2018

All things pass away, our time on earth is brief, and yet we may feel assailed at great length in this brief time, and yet we may reach moments of great happiness. All this so true it is only a truism to say so. Some people detest the modern habit of calling life a journey, and yet it *is* a *peregrinatio*, and played out on a semi-sacred *camino*, of sorts. Do you remember Peter Brook's film of Gurdjieff's *Meetings with Remarkable Men*? I suppose that is a dubious title nowadays – for where are the women in that? But we all may feel we have been a witness to some remarkable people along the way.

And now and then the most remarkable, even the most important, may be someone with the lowest evident social status – or none. I think of my great-aunt Annie, for whom I wrote a little novel, *Annie Dunne*, largely in an attempt to testify to her remarkable nature, if bitter as the crab-apples she prized on her favourite tree. A woman with a hunchback and therefore, in the mistaken and cruel thinking of her youth, a hundred years ago, considered unmarriageable; and further therefore, destined to be childless all her life. And yet when my sister and myself were put with her when we were little, on a tiny subsistence farm in Wicklow, while my father and mother went to London to seek work, she turned out to be, for a four-year-old boy and a six-year-old girl, a very philosopher and almost inventor of mothering. How she bound us to her and her own cousin Sarah, how she harboured us, how she protected us – how she taught us to look beyond our own noses to the extravagant beauties of the hens like ballerinas in the yard, the helmeted cock the angry king of all things. How in effect, almost without meaning to surely, she taught us to see *her*, in a way we had never seen anyone. How her solitary, turning, light-gathering, beautifully speaking self hovered for us in the damp Wicklow air like a revelation and the aquatint smudge of a human angel. How when we went, she and I, to the well for water, and we waited under the hawthorn for the great coin of liquid to clear after a neighbour's muddying of it, the zinc bucket creaking in the hook of her hand, and the fingertips of the rain touching and tipping our faces, I loved her with the open-hearted love of a rescued soul and a renewed child.

But in the eyes of the world, what was she? A spinster without monetary resources, without clothes beyond the two dresses she owned and darned and perpetually spruced up, and a polka-dot apron; with half of her cousin Sarah's narrow bed for a niche in the world of dreams, dependent not only on the kindness of strangers but that even more precarious kindness, the kindness of your kind.

Let's not pretend that the four-year-old boy remembers nothing and is not already a sort of writer, a writer that of course cannot actually write, and indeed I *couldn't* write as I have sometimes confessed till I was maybe eight. And that was because we followed eventually my mother and father to London, and in that exile – not from country exactly, but from Annie's soft influence, and the influence of my Barry grandfather, Matthew, whom I also loved far past idolatry – I must have minutely panicked at such baulks and tasks as writing. But a writer nonetheless, let's say who just never wrote, who was blocked from the get-go, so instead was noting and marshalling and itemising *in his swimming head* along the way. Otherwise I could not have written the little novel much much later. I could not have written it unless it was already written – on the air as may be.

At any rate I have tried to live by the example of that radiant woman all my life.

So we travel on and look for objective correlatives of individuals like herself, our *great* great-aunts, and all those who strained – in the constraints of their own adulthood perhaps – to provide a sense of safety and shelter to us as children. Which to my mind is the great purpose and ambition of the parent, to lend a cloak of security and a bright hiding place of safety to a child. Which I learned as a child, appropriately enough, in the first laboratory of things as provided by Annie in that long-ago, vanished, rescinded Wicklow locus. For in the manner in which she lived, no one now lives. Pony and trap, a milking cow, a pig to kill yearly, a few wet-nosed calves, an acre of wheat, a field of grass, stone mushrooms to guard her grain against rats, soft wild hand-dancing in the dairy to make the butter, proper functioning piseogs, menacing fairies, turf fires and all.

I speak of myself as a young writer then, aged four. And how at every age I have looked for, or been fortunate accidentally to find, what can we call them, avatars, or examples, or people of fundamental endurance – teachers in effect of not only how to write, since I would be obliged to write as well as I can anyway, but crucially, how to live – for I must live as well as I can, too, like anyone.

I accept there have been one or two conventionally 'famous' writers who have shown me, in their different ways, a class of indefatigable conduct and an apex of endurance, as if in some essential way we are always on what amounts to a strange war footing in life, not only as writers, but as beings who are merely alive. A war footing, even if the war thankfully seldom reaches us. The armies move along the landscape a few miles beyond the horizon. We hear of atrocities and sorrows in the distance, certainly. Let me not exclude here an avatar simply because he or she was lauded and maybe even burdened by the epithet 'great' while they lived. The great writer rises to the moment and in himself or herself can be nothing more than normal as bread – and yet will be expected to be otherwise and somehow holy. Who will face that inconvenience. And who will face the inconvenience, having been welcomed or not so welcomed into life, as may be, of finally leaving it again. This troubled and troubling figure called Death being neither really the guide or by corollary the destroyer we sometimes give him credit for being, but some class of figurative waterfall over which our little skiff must eventually launch itself, that little extra tug on our boat being felt many miles upriver as may be, and other than that, oftentimes giving no indication or warning; and therefore no preparation can be possible for our sudden flight into air and scattering water, with the bells and whistles of a myriad rainbows.

Some years ago the postman brought a letter the very envelope of which filled me with disquiet. The writing on it was in black ink and I thought I recognised the hand. I brought the letter to a chair in the garden and braced myself to read. We had not been getting on very well, this person and myself, and I was obliged to ready myself for whatever the letter might contain. I pulled out two full sheets of writing, and although the e's were not the Greek e's I was expecting, I still feared it. I started to read. It seemed to be about two of my novels and I was suddenly surprised and gladdened that this person was writing in such praising terms. Were we at peace at last? I discounted the lack of Greek e's in my delight. Surely a praiser's handwriting can be allowed to change? The writer had certainly looked into the novels deeply, and seemed grateful, with a proportionate depth, for the experience. The letter was elegant, generous and wonderfully composed. I read to the end, and there at the bottom was not the signature I expected. Written in full, because in person he was a stranger to me. Who lived so deeply and far away in effect I maybe thought nothing so ordinary as the post could bring that name into our house. I was so astonished I stood up, alone in the garden, but suddenly in a great crowd of thoughts – the reaction of the continuing child in me I suppose – and shook for a bit and then went into the house to look for Ali, my wife. By a piece of irony, she just so happened to be in the little space we call the laundry, actually on her knees in rather worrying Pinteresque fashion, I thought, in my addled way, and she paused kindly enough while I read her the letter, myself trembling still, overwhelmed, thrown into a state of happy stupidity, and only uttering the name at the end. Oh my God, she said. Exactly. The name, in that severe and very permanent black ink, was indeed Harold Pinter.

Some weeks later my friend and play editor Dinah Wood, being a magical person, arranged a lunch in London. Harold Pinter was so ill, I am bound to relate, it took him about twenty minutes to get from his car to the table. Moving so slowly he did not seem to be moving, like the arms of those huge new wind turbines on our nearby mountain in Wicklow. The two of us sat side by side, both of us a little deaf, and leaned in to talk our allotted nonsense and sense. It was very delightful and very strange, like an episode out of a young writer's dream, though I was fully fifty-three years old. Off he went, we dispersed, we went our separate ways.

Not so long after, he died. He had been very kind, very democratic in his sudden friendship, and very mysterious. Even in the extremity of an illness, he had thought it a good thing to write a long letter to a poor creature in Ireland he didn't know, about that creature's books. It was something he had seemingly been intent on doing, illness or no illness. It was an impulse he had not neglected to act on. To offer praise and friendship to another damn writer, even in what proved to be those signal things, his last days. It seemed to me an astonishing thing to do, and a thing full of meaning, even if, like most important meanings, it was elusive and more at the level of magic than anything else.

Annie Dunne to Harold Pinter. We must glean our wisdom where it lies, not where it is supposed or considered to lie. Like the gleaners in the eighteenth century, who went out after the harvest proper to take the last poor stalks of gold light from the ground.

If Death is gathering people to have them at his own table, then maybe the best we can say about him is, he has excellent taste in humanity. But we may curse his haste, his inhumanity and his crazy impudence, all the same.

Meetings with remarkable men and women. Let me talk about another person who thought their way into the circumstances of a young writer, as I then was, and made a highly pragmatic move to alter them.

Val Mulkerns was born, according to the data, in 1925, but she was perpetually stocked with youthfulness. This was the secret of the freshness of her writing. She seemed to lead a quiet and retiring life, but she was a person of very particular vision and opinion. In her memoir *Friends with the Enemy*, she is clear in her contempt for the rigid Catholicity of Eamon de Valera. She put her head above the parapet I suspect in a thousand conversations when it was perilous to do so, and worked on the famous contrarian magazine *The Bell* in the fifties when Seán Ó Faoláin and Anthony Cronin were editors. She was one of those writers who wanted to take Ireland by the scruff of the neck and demand maturity of it, a maturity we are even now still just inching towards.

When I was thirty-four and on the cusp of marrying – not that I *knew* that – she and her friend the Northern writer Ben Kiely conspired to get me into Aosdána. I am not even sure why they did it, they just seemed to make it their business. My father, a poet of her generation, admired and liked Val, and so I knew of her before I ever wrote a word myself. I think of that generation as sometimes harsh and even half ruined by existentialism and a sort of national despair. It must have been a horror to find yourself an intellectual in that Ireland. Yet she was an exception to that. She was the least despairing person.

In the eighties she published a novel called *The Summerhouse*, which I happened to review in the *Irish Times*, *very* enthusiastically. She wrote me a note and said she was glad my parents had gone to the trouble of conceiving me.

Her writing went right back into the 1950s. *A Time Outworn* was published in 1951 when she was in her mid twenties and got an admiring letter from Frank O'Connor, who then galvanised himself into promoting her in America. At that time O'Connor was the principal Irish writer of the day. What he noted in her work is still true sixty-seven years later.

Also in the seventies and eighties she published three collections of stories, including her masterpiece, *Antiquities*. For a time she was central in Irish letters in that curious and unfathomable habit of fashion and happenstance that literary fate goes in for. Some years before her Aosdána intervention, I remember being in the writers' retreat of Annaghmakerrig. When she arrived she had been allotted an attic room at the top of some rickety stairs, and I was luxuriating by mere luck in one of the bigger rooms. So we swapped. Not because of any noble instinct of mine, but because, well, she was Val Mulkerns. I remember being in awe even of the letters she received, arrayed on the hall table. From her eminent agent and her British publisher, bulwarks against indigence I was signally lacking myself. In that time there were none of the stupendous Irish fiction publishers that put electricity into the grid today.

Sometimes a writer can live a long time and seem therefore to outlive their allotment of fame. Whatever fame is. The admiration of the tribe? A just elevation? An error of understanding? Well, who knows. As a student of Latin at Trinity I did note the facts of the long game, and the accident of it all. At any rate, I suppose it is a pity we are not better able to celebrate and revere writers always when they are that bit older. In Ireland we have the indomitable examples of Jennifer Johnston and Edna O'Brien, so it is not always the case. Val's reputation had

been moved from the ballroom to the anteroom, certainly.
But I am not sure it bothered *her* very much. Last time I
drove her home to Dalkey, we were talking about writing,
and she said she was anxious to get going at something,
she felt there had been too great a gap. I offered the suggestion that she might justifiably rest another little while
on her perpetual laurels. She was definitely not keen on
that. On going into her house, in the confidence of her
ninety beautifully lived years, she offered the observation
that, as long as you didn't come down with a very serious
illness, why, you could live forever.

It was Ben Kiely who actually made the speech at Aosdána that got me elected. I was thirty-four as I say, the
youngest person elected up to that time, until an even
younger character in the person of radiant Dermot Bolger
got in some time later. Ben Kiely read a passage from the
last page of a wild novel I had written called *The Engine
of Owl-Light*. It isn't in print. The late Tony Cronin said
it was a lost masterpiece of Irish literature, which was
just like him – high words on behalf of a youngster. The
late Aidan Higgins ended his review with 'A wide sweep

of the uplifted hat – on, on!' Everyone else, in so far as it was noticed, said it was pants, and worse than that, pants that didn't fit. But Ben Kiely must have struggled through it, or at least the last page, which was quite possibly the best page. At least your ordeal was over. He read out the passage and declared, 'Anyone who writes like that is the company I want to keep.' The ears of the assembled members of Aosdána pricked up. I didn't know him at all, although I knew *Proxopera*, which was that rare bird, a hit novella, and *Nothing Happens in Carmincross*, which come to think of it was that equally rare thing, a hit novel.

We moved into a flat in North Great George's Street on the strength of their efforts and the resulting *cnuas*, the stipend that miraculously comes with membership. We needed it. Let me take a moment delicately to praise Charles Haughey who agreed to Tony Cronin's suggestion to invent a body that might support writers. After all, even Horace, Propertius and Virgil needed the mercy of Maecenas.

Anyway, it meant we, and indeed the landlord – a certain magisterial character called David Norris – didn't have to worry about the rent. Prior to this, in humbler lodgings in Little Jerusalem, Ali used to hide under the bed when the rent-lady came round. Not because we didn't like her, but because we did, and hated disappointing her. We were heating the flat with Ali's grandmother's fuel vouchers. Writers have to survive their pennilessness somehow. Ali's grandmother had been dead for two years.

Indeed it was in that same period of possibly happy indigence – writing seemed to be a task independent of actual funds as far as the force of it went, the happiness of it – that I received a letter from Revenue, telling me to attend their court in St Stephen's Green. Here, I remember, was an actual judge on a high dais, and a battery of lawyers and whatnot ranged at a further table. Out in the corridor I had sat with trembling business people, clutching briefcases and possibly also straws. When I was called in, the judge asked me what I had earned in the last year. Nothing, I said. But you are a writer, are you not? I am – I was writing all morning in fact and am really looking forward to getting back to it. When you say nothing, do you mean a thousand pounds, two thousand pounds? I mean nothing, I said. *Nothing will come of nothing, speak again.* You didn't make a tax return and you are obliged to do so, even if the amount is zero, he said. I will do so, I said. That is the law, he said – Let me not see you here again! *I hear, and is my heart not badly shaken?*

Then Val and Ben to the rescue. A few years after that, Ali fell pregnant. Ascended pregnant? Come to think of it, Dermot Bolger was somewhat mixed up in that. Ali and I had been trying for a baby for about seven years. Then Dermot got me playing soccer out on the astroturf pitch at Dublin airport. It was an eclectic group of players, mostly writers and used-car salesmen, the latter I should think doing rather better financially than the former, or I hope so. Anyway all that exercise seemed to shake things up somewhat, and suddenly Ali was pregnant. Just to emphasise the healthy and blithesome effect of soccer, it was twins. They were born in 1992 and my soccer career continued unabated for a few short years more, until frequent injury obliged me to retire. Every Friday night I would sneak away religiously. By the time the twins were eighteen months old, they would latch onto a leg each, and try and stop me going out. I had to walk the length of the hallway with a babby on each shoe – me lovingly dislodging them – but *determined to escape* . . . Perhaps it is not unrelated that my daughter Coral became a fierce Liverpool fan, watching every match from age nine in our distant old house in the Wicklow mountains, and is now a sports journalist with *Metro* online in London.

Val might have thought twice and not bothered herself with assisting a half-, a quarter-proven writer. Ben Kiely might have saved his powder for another brighter prospect. But the assistance of a writer is not just about books. It was the beginning of the most important thing I have done in my life, which was to have the responsibility of the babies – the twins, Merlin and Coral, and then five years later, Toby. It is true to say that being elected to Aosdána allowed me to become a father. A writer I already was, and I cannot imagine anything would have stopped me. But children. There is a financial fright in having children. There is a terror. The concern not to involve them in your elected pennilessness is great. Those jars of baby food don't come cheap. Nappies are unconscionably dear.

Years later, I must record, I saw Ben Kiely in a cafe in Wicklow. He was with a friend and minder and he was quite frail-looking in truth. I wanted to thank him for what he had done, but I held back. Like a fool, I held back. I didn't go down to him.

I went to CUS in Leeson Street, founded by Cardinal Newman as a feeder school for the new Catholic University on Stephen's Green. Father Gus Herlihy was principal in my time and taught English. He was a sort of 'genius teacher' really, that many writers acknowledge having. Milton's *Paradise Lost*, Thomas Kinsella's 'Another September'. He burned them into us. On one occasion instead of an essay he allowed me to submit a short story, the first thing I ever wrote. I remember so vividly the sense of freedom, of escape from the rigours of exegesis, for which I had no talent. Like many another writer, it was an English teacher who let the outlaw go. You have to try and get down to Mexico before Pat Garrett shoots you in the back, but a great teacher in a mysterious way *has* that back from the get-go.

In 1986, in Little Jerusalem, Father Herlihy happened to pass the door of the precarious flat where Ali and I were living. He looked dishevelled, distracted and strange, and indeed I was told later he had had a breakdown, one of the quondam penalties of genius. I didn't say a word to him, not wishing to disturb him. Or maybe afraid of what I saw. *Not young and not renewable, but man*, as Kinsella wrote. But I should have run after him and touched the hem of his garment, regardless.

Long before election to Aosdána, in my early twenties I happened to meet Thomas and Eleanor Kinsella. The two were standing together at some function in a manner I *noted* – a unit of being, possibly breathing at the same pace. At the same metrical measure. The iambics of love. She said on no account was I to go being a poet, it was much too hard a life. Thomas smiling enigmatically by her side.

Anyway, at school in CUS, there was a wondrous boy in my class called Vadim. He was one of the sons of James Plunkett the writer. Vadim and I had a little club, complete with homemade membership cards, called the Wolf Club, and every lunchtime we went down to St Stephen's Green and I suppose had appropriately wolf-ish adventures. Over one summer we exchanged chapters of a novel, sending the instalments on those small blue pages, their lines a darker blue, in those days universally used for letters. As if an Irish letter-writer by definition would not have too much to say. Vadim was *very* critical of my contributions and I think felt they were not up to his standard. I am sure he was right.

Anyway, he was quite a boy, that Vadim. His father at that time had just published *Strumpet City*, a title which inspired a strange glee in one of our other teachers, also a priest. He not very subtly intimated to us the meaning of *strumpet*, which, even when he further intimated with smirks and cackles, was beyond us. It was not a very lofty level of engagement with such a classic novel, I suppose. At home my father had the issue of *The Bell*, published in 1954 and edited with a preface by Tony Cronin, that had published James Plunkett for the first time in book form, *The Eagles and the Trumpets*. Tony Cronin, himself only twenty-four at the time, begins his preface in Ciceronian measure: 'Anybody may write a preface to the dead, all that are needed being enthusiasm and a little style; an introduction to the living is a different matter.' James Plunkett was thirty-four. That little book's fire still hasn't gone out. It is true that there has been a number of Irish fiction renaissances, it's just the older ones get replaced. The new city is built on the ruins of the old. I still have that issue. It cost 2/6. I suppose it is worth a little more now. Its spiritual worth was always – immeasurable.

One day Vadim brought me home. He lived in Terenure. When we entered his house, modest and modern, we heard the strains of music from one of the rooms. I looked in through the crack of the door at two people there, who paid me no heed. At first I thought the man was dancing, his arms held up like the branches

SEBASTIAN BARRY

of Aunt Annie's crab-apple tree, stirring in the wind. It was James Plunkett and his wife, playing the viola and the piano together. Mrs Plunkett was smiling up at him, laughing without making the sound of laughter. It was a vision of domestic harmony – literally – that I was not privy to, say, at home. Our house was large, old and echoing and it was rare to meet anyone, and anyway no one played the piano or the viola. And certainly not together. I am still standing there at the door, looking in, eleven or twelve, entranced. I knew what I was looking at was important, but of course couldn't have said why. Avatars to be effective don't even have to notice you at the door.

Just saying this now I think of Blake and his wife, sitting in their apple tree, although Mr and Mrs Plunkett of course were fully clothed.

When Val and Ben Kiely got me into Aosdána, I was similarly entranced to go along to the first meeting. Many of the august faces I didn't know, the painters, the composers, even the writers. The faces of artists are often a document of their struggles. Palimpsest upon palimpsest, a biography of sorts. But one face thrilled me to behold. It was the same James Plunkett, now some twenty years older, characteristically moving along the room at a seemingly different speed and even in a different world

– 28 –

than everyone else. About strange deep business maybe. He belonged to a post-revolutionary era in Ireland but was a lamp for any present time. I admired him so much it gave me a headache to see him. Not too long after that he said something lovely about my work in an interview. To go from the viola to the sweet violence of praise seemed a long journey.

Years later yet again, I saw him in Bray. I didn't know why he was there, far from Terenure anyhow. He was going along more slowly, his old pace modified, entirely alone, and again, like Father Herlihy, looking somewhat *distrait* and distracted. He was frail too, concentrating mightily on crossing the road without injury, and here I am saying again, I didn't greet him, I didn't say hello. Of course, it occurs to me as I say this, I didn't *know* him, I had never actually had a conversation with him. It was all at a curious distance, and the distance was unbridgeable in the upshot.

So, seemingly, three great sins of omission, one might say. Ben Kiely, Father Herlihy, James Plunkett. But just because I failed in those instances didn't mean I didn't love those people. I revered them. Their good words and their good offices had given me a life, and given Ali and me a place, a site to have our babies and do our work.

Perhaps I am finally, just now, running after them.

When you are young there is a sort of ache to get on –
even, if we are being truthful, to get *above*. To get up onto
the drier ground, anyhow. I left Trinity when I was twenty-
two and promptly became, in great secrecy, a writer. For
many years I was published and even praised, but I had
no money. The problem of money in the writer's life.
Patrick Kavanagh said they don't want writers to be talking about money because they don't want to give them
any. I think of the beneficent good indeed that the *cnuas*
would have rendered to Kavanagh, standing outside his
house with a borrowed sixpence in his hand, and wondering whether to put it in the gas meter or buy a glass
of whiskey. Some years ago the eminent economist Colm
McCarthy said there was no need for the state to subvent
writers, because they will write anyway. This conjures up
the image of a sort of predetermined state of literary en-
deavour, peopled by strange creatures immune to money.
There's something in it, and nothing in it. After all, we
might say the same of economists – they don't need to be
paid because they will what, *economise*, anyway. Hardly.

To give him his due, I have known writers who seemed to be natural occurrences, like robins and their songs, or wrens. I think of Michael Hartnett, a man so unusual, so concentrated, that he was like a piece of the seventeenth century broken off and rendered into a gold coin. He wrote many truly great poems, none more so than 'Death of an Irishwoman', about his beloved grandmother who reared him, but which is also about pennilessness as it happens, among other things –

She was a child's purse, full of useless things.

It is those useless things that novels and plays and poems are made out of. Perhaps that was what Colm McCarthy was objecting to, paying for useless things like that. Things that great souls are made out of too. Michael Hartnett. Did I say he was a gold coin? Maybe a farthing is better, a coin indeed with a wren on it, in the old money. A poet so quick, so restless, so loved, so *awaited*. And only briefly here, a bird alighting on the field of life as if just *for a blessed moment*. At a handclap, off he flew. Even I, who did not know him as a close friend, relished him and in my secret heart celebrated my acquaintance with him. It was *delicious* to know him, even as he seemed to row himself ever quicker towards that bloody waterfall. Fiercely, fiercely.

———

When I heard about my election to Aosdána I happened to be in Annaghmakerrig. The playwright Tom Murphy arrived the same day in his BMW car – that impressed the hell out of me, or maybe just filled me with a sort of hope. It was an old BMW but it was still a Beamer. Tom himself seemed very friendly but quite sardonic and just at that time I don't think he was too content with how things were going generally in his career. Of course he was one of the best playwrights that had ever lived, the equal in my mind, and because I was young, almost of the same antiquity, as the Roman playwrights I had read at Trinity. One day we sat in the sun together outside that old house of Tyrone Guthrie's and he said he thought maybe writing wasn't worth all the trouble. It was probably too late for him, but – he could save a younger man. He had heard me singing and said maybe I should give up the writing and go on the road. Much more fulfilling. It was *The Gigli Concert* in 1983 – indeed a play about the power of singing – that had made me want to write a play. It dismayed me that he thought, that he was obliged to think even for a moment, that the business wasn't worth the candle in the upshot. But when he heard I had just been elected to Aosdána, he stood up and shook my hand. Don't worry about anything, he said. That's the best thing I've heard all year. He seemed old to me, but he also seemed young, going from gloom to delight in a heartbeat. He was in fact fifty-five. There was no reputation at the time greater than his. He was the apothecary for a thousand Irish ills. And yet he was doubtful.

It is partly the lack of money but also a much stranger thing, a sort of force that storms against the actual body of the artist. There is an attrition rate that is sometimes even visible. Ali and I lived on North Great George's Street for seven years by mercy of the *cnuas*. The poet and novelist Philip Casey lived the other side of O'Connell Street in a small house his father had bought for him and he often came over to visit us. How can I describe to you the gentle intensity of that man, his lovely honesty, his country courtesy? How funny he was, how scrupulous in the matters of the heart and the soul? How he never gave offence in his conversation, and who bore offence indeed with a sort of kingly indifference. I'd go down and wait for him at the corner of Parnell Street. I would glimpse his body swinging on his crutches in the distance, fiercely, through the endless light of summer evenings, through the tormenting dark of winters. Why he didn't just use his angelic wings was beyond me. His shock of thick hair like a kindling fire. When he shook my hand I always had to *beg him* to remember not to crush it, he had such a mighty grip. He wrote the Bann trilogy, three *riverlike* novels, one might say, and many many lovely poems that I lovingly and fiercely recommend to you. He wrote against the odds, he wrote without thought of surrender.

Philip was often in hospital for long stretches. Last December I was coming back from Paris. I had heard that he was in the hospice in Blanchardstown. I wanted to email him to let him know I would be dropping by on my way home from the airport, but I sent it at the last possible minute because I didn't want him to say no. I had been warned by Dermot that he might say no.

The nurse at the desk said Philip was in room 8 upstairs. So I went up, with that nervy bounce a hospital can induce. The doors into the rooms were glass and I peered into room 8, but there was only an old geezer in there, looking forlorn at his own bedside. No sign of our Philip. I went down and asked the nurse was she sure he was in room 8, there seemed to be another man in there. No, she said, that's Philip's room. So I traipsed back up and of course it was Philip, in his extremity. He was mid-thought as I came in but he rose like a boy and hugged me. *Ah, Sebastian.* I was so glad I had come. *Dear, dear Philip.* As sweet to each other as brothers. We talked for a few hours and then off I went as blithe as a starling, satiated with his company. In his next email he talked of the *History of Ireland* he was writing – the whole damn thing, he said, I will need another ten years because there's an awful lot of bloody history in this country and I plan to finish it, let me tell you. A few weeks later I emailed again and asked him how he was and he said he had made it home for Christmas. Hurray! A few weeks after that I asked again how he was and I got a short an-swer from which, even in email form, the pain and the anguish arose. Then he was gone.

———

Well, yes, it all passes. I won't be the first damn fool to notice that. Einstein said we don't have the sufficient amount of senses to understand that time is not even as we conceive it. All things, he said, are happening always, everywhere. There is no such thing as narrative time. So much for fiction.

This dying. Let me close with another stupendous woman, Leland Bardwell. She was a terrific writer. She was an unstoppable writer. *Girl on a Bicycle* is a most extraordinary book. Our old landlord David Norris has called it the best big house novel of the twentieth century.

She, in the early eighties, was instrumental in publishing my first book, a novella, *Macker's Garden*, with the Irish Writers' Co-op – an early version of something as magical, say, as today's Tramp Press. So we had got to know each other, in that easy way I thought was usual but I see now was not – she *engendered*, she *engineered*, friendship. She was the Isambard Kingdom Brunel of literary bridges. Born into an Anglo-Irish family, the Hones, full of painters and dignitaries, she nevertheless lived mostly on the crumbling margins of society and society's economies, at that hem where everything starts to fray, and economic theories flounder, where maybe she could work best, or perhaps where writing and having children had placed her. A couple of years after publishing the novella, she phoned me and asked would I like to help her to exercise some polo ponies. She was an expert horsewoman. She was moonlighting as it were at a little stables near Sandymount Strand, owned by some wealthy person. When I got there – it must have been a Saturday – she was standing in the dark of one of the stalls, and I soon saw that she was crying. I had had a poem in the *Irish Times* that morning. 'I've just read your poem,' she said, 'and now look at me.'

Anyway we saddled up two of the polo ponies and headed off to the strand to exercise them. Now polo ponies, I will tell you, just in case it is ever helpful, must never be galloped. If they get a taste for galloping they will move too quickly on the polo ground and run out across the boundaries – and possibly not be seen again. Leland in her gay and contented way instructed me in this as we clopped along. Even if you were never on Sandymount Strand, you will know it from *Ulysses*, and eternity does *still* seem to hover there. I knew it as a child, walking from the environs of Monkstown where we lived, all the way round to Ringsend, looking for pram wheels on the dump there that might serve as wheels for a go-cart.

On we went, talking about nothing and everything, poetry and family, and possibly prams. I was just back from a disastrous year in Switzerland, broken relationship, shattered dreams and all. I was back at home and miserable, as hypochondriacal and as mildly crazy as you like. Leland never minded things like that in a person. If she liked you, she rested her faith in you, she didn't need you to be anything but the self you were able to present that day. As such she was a deep deep pleasure to be with.

We reached the edge of Joycean eternity as it were, and headed out on the wide strand, skirting along those deep tidal rivers that cross and cross again when the sea is out. The tide doesn't just go out on Sandymount, it emigrates to England and then comes back dangerous and disgruntled. There is everywhere a sense of imminent flood, erasure, danger. Which suited us down to the ground. Suddenly, gradually, suddenly, whatever was bothering her that day was falling away, and whatever was bothering me likewise. We just ever so slightly opened up the ponies, and went cantering delicately towards the tiny long line of the sea on the horizon. Cargo ships out there looked like mere balsa-wood hovercraft on the shimmering acres. The gulls didn't mind us, the sand drummed back at us. You might as well call those ponies Caribbean musicians. I was up in my stirrups now because in truth we were gathering speed. Then Leland rose like a veritable jockey and let out a great cry, and gave her pony his head, and off she streaked like the

loudest and nicest banshee that ever was in Ireland. Her
hair she always wore wild but this was wildness beyond
wildness. Eternal Leland! I roused my pony after. We galloped like souls that had never known such happiness.
We hallooed and we caterwauled. Her whole body was
laughing. We wept for damnable joy. We ran those ponies
off the very pitch of Ireland and I don't know if they were
ever good for polo again. And I would apologise to the
unknown owner, except – I cherish that day when Leland
and I finally won our Irish freedom.

———

At sixty-three myself writing this, I have been working
for forty-one years. I am keeping an eye on the time, *pace*
Einstein. Part of the reason I accepted the laureateship
in such high excitement was just that. It has been a long
time, but like all time looked back on, it seems to barely have dimension. A private Bayeux tapestry but even a
long, long tapestry has only the depth of a communion
wafer. What remains true is, I have been privileged to
encounter some extraordinary souls, yes – but it is the
accidental, impromptu nature of it that impresses me.
Idle friendships, people thrown together, and sometimes

never a suspicion that not only was it adding to the value of my life, but actually in the upshot constituted that value. Avatars, guides, exemplars, headed up by the avatar in chief, my ordinary, hunchbacked great-aunt Annie, before time was even time.

I have laboured even to begin to understand the world, since I have been obliged, and even privileged let us say again, to visit it, just like anyone. I think it has behoved me to do that. But I couldn't but have stumbled in the dark without my secular avatars, without my own *versions* of them, written on the heart, scribed on the soul. They may not even be true versions. But even the errors will have served me. It might be all luck and happenstance but it has led me betimes into marble halls. I think of these figures every day, I refer to them like texts or aphorisms, I live by them, I live sometimes through them, and I live towards them, even unto the waterfall.

STILL LIFE, WITH DONAL

Second Laureate Lecture

Given at the Gate Theatre, Dublin
6 October 2019

This lecture began with the singing of a few lines from 'Tears in Heaven', by Eric Clapton and Will Jennings, which was a favourite song of Donal McCann's during his last illness.

It's another life.

We're living in North Great George's Street. It's 1994. David Norris is our benign landlord and has been for five years. Being elected to Aosdána in 1989 had finally allowed us consistently to pay rent, which has been a great boon. Another boon, in the shape of the curious tornado, the wonderful catastrophe, that was the birth of twins, has come in 1992, asking probing questions nonetheless about our vulnerable economy. Ali has stopped working as an actress to give all her time and self to those babies. I have had a play put on in London for the first time, in the year of their birth, but after a short canter at the Bush Theatre and then at the Peacock in Dublin, that has contributed only its modest halfpence. But we're not downhearted, and in truth we know no better. Personally at this time I think it will always be so, leaping stepping stone by stepping stone across the wide stormy isthmus of a working life. I hope one day to buy a broken cottage in Mayo and for us all to live frugally there. That seems a perfectly admirable and justifiable life, if a little uncertain for the babies.

The year after the children's coming has been a new sort of time. So many things have changed. It's not just myself and Ali battling along, shoring each other up (she does most of such shoring). There has also been the strange ballet of the babies' sleeping, or not sleeping so much, for the first seven months, or at least sleeping according to their own mysterious rules. It has been a mighty see-saw in and out of bed for their novice parents. First baby up, merry and hungry, feed the critter, back down to sleep, and then the little leg of second baby stirring, lifting, in the cot. Second baby, merry and hungry for a stretch. Then sleeping. First baby's leg lifting again . . .

There have been times in the dark night in North Great George's Street when we have passed them to each other like rugby balls. With the vigour of a good Irish forward.

Even, in the deep crease of sleeplessness, when we have cursed, if not them, then each other. We had spent seven years together with barely a cross word (as I remember it). Now we perfected a few insults in the cold crucible of the night. One of the best we memorialised and often repeated later – 'You piece of human excrement.' Which of us fashioned that, I can't recall. Bleary-eyed, I would wheel them out into the dawn, to allow them to take the air in the Royal Canal Basin, and Ali to sleep, to sleep. She was breastfeeding like a champion – indeed also like a curious rugby player, except running with two ovals at the same time.

We were well-nigh paralysed by exhaustion.

Then we moved the twins' cot into my old workroom at the back of the flat and I bought two child-rearing books, one American and one English. The English one said you had to go in when your baby cried at night, it would be un-British not to do so. The American one said that the father should hover at the door looking through the keyhole and let the baby cry the first night, that it would be less the second night, that mama should not be allowed to go in, and that soon, soon, your baby would be sleeping 'like all the other babies in the neighbourhood'.

I went with the Yankee book.

The first night indeed I did not sleep myself, but stood watchman at the door. When one child cried, Ali appeared all cloaked in sleepiness. If her arms had been outstretched like a sleepwalker I would not have been surprised. Each time she appeared, speechless and answering an ancient imperative, I turned her gently around in the corridor and nudged her back towards her bed.

That first night Coral cried for forty minutes, then stopped. I could see her twisting the surface of the sheet tinily, teaching herself to sleep. The next night Merlin cried for fifteen minutes. 'It's OK, Ali, turn around, back you go . . .' Then the third night, an epochal silence. Sleeping babies. I set up the monitor and climbed into bed. At six, I woke like a creature re-doused in humanity. A night's sleep! Would I ever experience it again? Oh wonder, the same the next night. Miraculous.

Now when the older ladies on O'Connell Street peered into the buggy and remarked on how delightful the twins were – 'Ah, Jaysus, aren't they just lovely,' I didn't nod and privately think, *but they have ruined our lives*, but now nodded and spoke aloud in wondering agreement. Delightful. Champion babies. Champion sleepers.

God bless America.

In the era of the sleeplessness I had been trying to fulfil a play contract for Max Stafford-Clark at the Royal Court, that he had commissioned in the utterly different days before the babies. He had seen the halfpenny-earning Bush play and thought he might like to commission me. That was a happy day.

I met him in his office in the Court. As I came in he was talking to someone on the phone, clearly a tricky conversation.

'That,' said Max, setting the receiver back down, 'was Edward Bond. Sends a play every year. Always have to turn him down.'

I nodded in youthful ignorance of this most likely fate of older playwrights. I was thirty-seven and Max was not turning me down. The necessary stupidity of thirty-seven. Oh yes, we spoke about what I thought I wanted to do, a strange play about a great-grandfather who had been chief superintendent of the old Dublin Metropolitan Police before independence, with three daughters and a son lost in the First World War. Max had just done a *King Lear*-like play somewhere in the English provinces, so this appealed to him. I left his office still marginally sorry for Edward Bond, but of course hugging my own good fortune, hurried down into Sloane

Square and banged into a phonebox, rang Ali – *he wants to commission it!*

Then the babies, then the sleepless nights.

And I tried to write the play, sleep or no sleep, but I began to realise something. The reason you have something coherent to write in the morning is because you have been preparing it somehow in dreams the night before. But if you have no space for dreams and sleep, you will write a very curious and very very useless subtext or supertext or some damn thing that is *not a play*.

Then the Yankee baby book, then suddenly sleep, then suddenly the play came. Almost whole and entire, it was a matter of writing it down. And not in a way very useful to Ali. I would be working in our bedroom, since the babies had evicted me, and only a few minutes after I would go in and close the door, it seemed, she would knock and say, 'Please, please, come and help me with the babies.'

'But I've only been here a moment!'

'Bear, Bear' (for that was my nickname), she would say, 'it's been eight hours!'

Scandalous. And so the play was written.

The fabulous juggling with babies continued. I delivered the play to Max and then went again to London to talk about it. He was fairly enthusiastic. Not hugely.

'You talked about it better than you wrote it,' I seem to remember him saying. I was happy to take the temperature he was lending it, because I had no great expectations. I had read the play to Ali in bed and she had said, after a few pages, 'This is something new for you.' So this 'new' had to be encountered and understood. As always, it might be a pile of malodorous nonsense. You just have to leave room for that possibility.

I did some work on the play and sent it off again (by *post*, a *typescript*, in an *envelope*) and then there was a certain amount of silence, a certain kind of silence. The silence of uncertainty the other end. Max was just coming to the end of his time at the Royal Court as artistic director, oftentimes triumphant, oftentimes tempestuous. He was there but not there, in the manner of prime ministers and presidents at the end of their offices.

Then he wrote to me and said he didn't think he could direct it and would give it over to the new people at the Court and in due course I heard that one of the directors would give it a rehearsed reading but that he thought it was 'a pretty static' play. This moved me to tell my agent to say that I wanted her to take the play back. In the same moment I rang Max and asked him, if he couldn't direct the play, could he at least 'look after it' at the Court. I'm not sure what I meant, except I could sense I was now occupying that difficult but familiar niche, the halfpenny place, and was no doubt standing on my dignity as a method of surviving that. You have to try and protect the tiny centre of confidence or other more permanent dooms await. The strange pride of the beggar-man. But Max immediately said he would, yes, he would look after it, certainly, in a sudden rush of comradeship.

I remember walking in my father-in-law's little wood in Mayo and thinking, well, bugger this for a profession, would it be too late now to join the army, as my grandfather had urged me? The British army indeed. The merciless and unfathomable exchange of hatreds burned and roared ever deeper and longer in the North, so it was in every way a crazy thought. But the halfpenny place is a great prompter to absurdity. I was thinking of the price of nappies, of baby food, of baby clothes, of crèches, of schools, of possible ponies, of universities, of . . . And of my apparent inability, so far, to do anything but write, even if it was just to write pretty static plays.

From that point on something a little mysterious

happened. Max seemed more and more inclined not only to look after *The Steward of Christendom*, but to take it to himself. He was setting up a new theatre company with Sonia Friedman called Out of Joint. Some twenty years before he had worked with an Irish actor called Donal McCann, and he thought he might just send the script to Donal. What did I think? I said, yes, please do.

But with private misgivings. Donal McCann. I knew he was a great drinker and I was not a fan of drinkers, in the main. My grandmother had drunk herself to death, my grandfather narrowly escaped that when he gave it up in the fifties, my father was a drinker ... When I mentioned Donal's name in Dublin, some said, with that special tone reserved for complicated rivalries among actors, that his work had grown 'mannered'. Hmm. I had some tricky memories of encountering Donal myself. Once in the Abbey foyer I had seen him crawl vertically along a wall, if that is possible – using the wall for a reference as if the entire Abbey were pitching in a great tempest. I suppose his life was a great tempest, mostly. I thought it was a sorrowful sight. For Donal was blatantly an actor of singular greatness. It was just the drinking, the drinking, the astonishing and old-fashioned drinking. Tales of him drinking all day in a certain bar, and being locked into the premises by the barman at night, with twenty double vodkas lined up for him on the counter. The peculiar murderous kindness of a barman. Then him being released at dawn, and down to the markets with him, where the bars opened for the starlit traders. Drinking of a kind I wonder does it even exist now, in that many many drank like that, many Irish artists, actors, writers. The lost drinkers of the twentieth century. I think of it as wild grown-up drinking of a kind so beyond me I feel almost ashamed to admit it. Manly, womanly, epic, Irish drinking, giving rise to wonder tales and catastrophes just averted. But I was *familiar* with stories like those, literally, in my own family, and was also aware of the scars and horrors visited on those around the drinker. No, I was not a fan of it, or of drinkers, and maybe so didn't really want him in my play. My pretty static play. Also, he was only fifty-two, and the character of Thomas Dunne was in his early seventies. Could even a Donal McCann make that leap? I was worried, I was worried. Though I knew behind all this, in the dark anteroom of reason, that I was looking a gift horse in the mouth, and anyway, he mightn't want to do it. This was the man who had specialised in Sean O'Casey and Brian Friel after all, and Anton Chekhov as translated by Friel.

But I did remember some other things now. Meeting Donal one time in a cramped pub on a street called the Hill, behind North Great George's Street, accidentally, him coming into the bar with his grungy regality, standing suddenly – always sudden, though he moved not – beside me, saying nothing, saying nothing, till he announced, in his conversation-murdering way, 'I'm afraid of you.' (Not an iota of fear in his voice.)

'Why so?' I said, appalled, affrighted.

'I'm afraid of you, I'm afraid of you,' he said, as if repeating it would make it clearer what he meant.

'Well,' I said, in a mix of genuine fright and dubious arrogance, 'I hope some day we will work together, you and I.'

'Humph!' he said, with maximum ambiguity.

He managed to get little messages to me over the years, in that Dublin grapevine way. 'Donal McCann says that *Prayers of Sherkin* [another play of mine in 1990] is a masterpiece.' Oh, I thought, did he say that? How bloody wonderful.

In the time that Ali and I lived in David Norris's house, with the babies – the first babies born on the street for forty years, we were told, by lovely epic Patty Duffy in her shop on Parnell Street – we were in the era of BM – Before Mobiles – and we still relied mainly on the squatting phone in the sitting room. One afternoon this creature stirred and I answered and it was a gruff Dublin voice on the other end:

'You've been stealing my childhood stuff off the radio. You've been listening to me talking on the radio about my childhood and you've robbed it!'

This said with proper force and burning accusation, as you might in a violent court case.

'Who is this?' I said, in my best South Dublin tone, neither revealing that I was offended or at the same time borrowing his venom.

There was a long breathing pause, and then a strange laughter, not the laughter of people at ease together, but an altogether different, private, singular laughter.

'It's Donal!'

Then I was searching in my mind for Donals I knew, I didn't think it was ever gentle Donal O'Kelly, who had been in *Prayers of Sherkin*, and anyway maybe I knew who this was, and my slow brain – always brotherly when it comes to stupidity – even my slow brain was putting two and two together.

'Oh, Donal,' I said, '*Donal*,' as if the word Donal was the answer to some complicated mathematical equation worthy of William Rowan Hamilton walking along the Royal Canal and suddenly scratching the principle of quaternion multiplication on a bridge, $i^2 = j^2 = k^2 = ijk = -1$, thereby many years later allowing a rocket to reach the moon, and there was a triumph in saying it: '*Donal!*'

'Meet me in the Step-down Inn at three tomorrow,' he said, with a suddenly conspiratorial tone, in, as it were, perfect friendship now – now that the theft of his childhood material had been mentioned, put in the open and dealt with.

Let's be clear. Ali and I revered him.

The Step-down Inn was only a few yards from our basement gate on North Great George's Street, and Donal as it happened stepped first down our stairs to collect me on the appointed day, and no doubt put his immortal hand out to ring our bell, and on the door being opened, came into our dark corridor, and was briefly in the hall. I was kerfuffling about to get ready, and he had a few Donalesque words with Ali, who had worked many times in the Abbey Theatre, and indeed had played the lead in *Prayers of Sherkin* (beautifully). Then he turned about and went back up to the street to wait for me. Ali gripped my arm, or did I grip hers, and said, or did I say, 'Donal McCann was in our house!' Either way, that was the degree of reverence we had for him, and the measure of our awe.

Just to be clear.

The radio interview reference was duly explained. It was his way of emphasising the connection he had made in the synapses of his own mind with the country matters in the play. The hens, the eggs, the cow, the calves, the dog, the pony and trap, the high lamp to light you along the green roads and the metalled ways, in the old gone blazing days of memory. We sat there among the local drinkers, some of them with their children playing outside on the pavement, waiting for ma and da in the dusky sunlight, and talked together for about two or three hours. Although I have no medals for being relaxed in human company, I was a version of relaxed with him, because anyway, he was talking directly into the very heart of my private imagination.

He was setting us up as strange brothers, or maybe a more filial arrangement, he assumed a sort of familiar connection in which he never wavered. Whether it was real, true or accurate was not the point. He was doing it to connect himself to this play he was going to do, even though I doubt he was ever, during rehearsals, 100 per cent sure it would work on stage. There was something in it he thought he needed, some corroboration of his own secret self – of course a secret self that he was always prepared to reveal in the strange public privacy of the stage.

I knew immediately he was the most serious hombre I had ever spoken to. If I wasn't terrified, I was at least elevated into an extreme watchfulness or concentration. He wasn't like an actor as such, with the fears and attributes of an actor. He had a sort of shamanistic certainty to him, an absoluteness, a one-time-only, the-most-important-thing-on-earth-is-good-writing atmosphere about him. To sit with him in those circumstances was to feel the hoops of a kind of steely love being bound about your person, and you were grateful for that, if also *constricted*. His growling, gravelly Dublin voice, hewn out of the smoke of a million cigarettes, with its faithful homage to a vanished Brendan Behan, and a thousand and one nights drinking, that utterly grown-up drinking as I said that I knew I would never be eligible to attempt.

I had never met anyone like him, nor ever did again.

He was drinking what he now called a 'Donal

McCann', half Britvic orange and half fizzy water, in a pint glass. Not a drop of alcohol in it. In fact, he had recently done the voiceover for the ad for Ballygowan, though that might have been coincidental. Much to my surprise, he had been dry for three or four years. Maybe this was a different Donal then. It was 1994, deep in the year, and we were to start rehearsals in London in March.

'Still life – Ballygowan – no other water.'

No other Donal.

Donal may have been fifty-three but his hair knew nothing about it. He had dense black thick hair, capping his head like a protective helmet, cut close, like on the Greek statue of an athlete. His main expression was one of concentration and a general fierceness. He had by some life alchemy turned a permanent frown into an appealing glare. He was not sartorially inclined. His trews were more or less a defrocked priest's idea of casual wear, he inclined to a tatty jumper over a shirt of long service. This was rehearsal room garb, and over the years it has been interesting to me to observe what actors wear to work, as it were. There is something in the degree of downplaying your clothes that relates to the up-playing of the text. If you wear the least of your items, the gods might favour you with those inches and ashes and sparks of discovery.

It was my first time working with Max Stafford-Clark, and although we went on to try to push out three other plays, I think he might agree this was the heyday of our connection. Max, and indeed Donal too, always put me in mind of those Russian icon makers who were content simply to honour their gods by painting them well, and not stoop to signing the icons. Real work in the theatre, those real hours composed of extraordinarily compressed moments, planetary, burning, alert, brings out the best in its great artists. You are in the presence of the individual at their most sublime. This is just a fact. Tina Kellegher played the part of Annie in *The Steward of Christendom*, in effect a younger version of my own great-aunt Annie, my favourite person on earth as a child, even my grandfathers coming second to her. Tina, like Donal, didn't come into the play to discharge the duty of a part and then go home. She was as focused as the arrows of Cupid, she was about that mysterious business of striking into the human heart without wounding it, which is the business of great acting. I mention her because it often seemed in the following years that only

Donal McCann was in that play. And yet there was a cast of seven or eight. Slowly during rehearsals the crucible of Max and Donal refined and condensed their efforts into beautiful work – condensed like stars both collapsing and expanding, it mattered not which. That was true. But there were other miracles. Playing the mostly unpleasant orderly, Smith, who at one point brings a bowl of stew for Thomas, was Kieran Aherne, who was not only liked by Donal but, more importantly maybe, had himself an acute understanding of Donal's sometimes astringent mood on stage. Kieran gave Donal carte blanche in the matter of moods and both absorbed and ignored everything, as it served the play. As a reward Donal truly liked him as I say, even if sometimes, when Kieran was radiantly reading out the old letter from the trenches that the Steward's son had sent him years before, Donal would mutter, in that strange stage communication between actors, that audiences can't for some reason hear, 'Hurry up!'

Perhaps his final reward for this majesty and patience was Donal's inspired description of Kieran – 'the man who put the stew into *The Steward of Christendom.*'

But the main astral physics was going on between Donal and Max. Donal considered Max to be the greatest living English theatre director. Max privately opined to me that in fact he had to believe that, because otherwise Donal could not have come to work with him again. They had worked together twenty years before on Tom Kilroy's translation of *The Seagull*, and this was why Max had felt he could send *The Steward* to Donal in the first place. Twenty years in the theatre can seem like an afternoon to its practitioners, and Donal had maintained his high opinion of Max for its strange duration.

Max was famous for what is called his 'actioning', which comprises himself and the actor working out an active verb for every sentence in the part. This verb is then noted in your script and referred to as required. It is Max's way of anchoring the actor and lightly pinning the text to a sort of rescuing sense.

Donal dutifully, manfully, respectfully sat down the other side of the rehearsal table on the first day and gamely, nobly, seriously, generously began this process with Max, and I am trying to remember how long this lasted, but I would be surprised if it went beyond an hour. Donal couldn't work like that partly because his part was composed of many long speeches, and perhaps in the upshot there was only one active verb for each entire speech.

And he had not learned his part as such before rehearsal. But for a very good reason. He didn't allow himself to. He wanted to let it 'learn itself', he wanted the surprises and mysteries of that osmosis. He had sat with the script for a thousand hours already, in his little house in Glasnevin, where he lived with his partner Fedelma Cullen (the gentlest woman in Ireland). The script was scrawled in, neatly written on, much coffee-cupped, or maybe tea-cupped, scuffed, folded, no doubt when he had stuffed it into his outrageously elderly leather jacket – like all his clothes obliged to do permanent service, as if a man could by law only ever purchase one jacket per life. It was thrilling for a writer to go to this house, in the months before rehearsal, as an extension of the programme begun in the Step-down Inn, in fact for the veritable cross-pollination between his imagination and mind and your own – and view this ferociously attended-to document – *which you had written* – thrown carefully to his side on the couch, as he variously watched the races at Sandown or the Curragh or wherever the horses were running that day, threw remarks back over his right shoulder to Fedelma who might be scanning the papers at their table, or offered to me his opinions of things he was reading – Colum McCann's tiny story 'Fishing the Sloe-black

River', about mothers fishing for their sons, being a discovery I remember him expounding on for a space much longer than the actual story. It was utterly thrilling.

Even to go to his house and not find him there yet was an adventure. I remember wandering into the old graveyard while waiting for him and finding myself not among the heroes of 1916, who were there somewhere, eternally, but among the heroic souls of the Angels' Acre, the little plot for babies and children, the continuing love for whom was marked by rainy teddy bears and dewy flowers. It was as if to be in the vicinity of – near the village of – Donal brought revelations in and of itself. I also knew that somewhere in the graveyard was the unmarked grave of my great-grandfather, no one knew where – the very man we were seeking to disinter in the theatre.

These many hours spent together had completed a certain sort of work for him. Now he was going fishing with Max, even if Max was suddenly obliged to take a new tack as regards actioning. So I was both required and redundant, but both conditions with a positive charge. Max was keen for the writer to be there every day of rehearsal, which meant six weeks in London, Ali and the babies at home in Dublin. Ali lifting, sorting, feeding, changing, herding, cajoling, teaching, amusing those babies, and thankfully, getting them to sleep at night for the rescue of her own dreams.

Although I had been made a member of Aosdána and we could pay our rent as a consequence, as I say, nevertheless money was tight. Nappies and jars of baby food are dear. I suppose there must have been a rehearsal stipend from Out of Joint – Max's producer, the majestic Sonia Friedman, didn't expect her writers to live on air – but we were rehearsing to go into a space with only sixty seats, the Theatre Upstairs at the Royal Court. Even if we managed to make the play 'go', no one was going to get rich.

As a consequence Donal after rehearsal would always enquire where I was going to get my dinner and if I occasionally didn't seem 100 per cent sure, he would shove a few quid into my hand and I would go and get a reviving McDonald's. At the weekend he had me come over to his modest digs in immodest Chelsea. Donal had many attributes. He loved drawing, he loved taking photographs, he loved to do the occasional bit of journalism, he was obviously the King of all Kings among actors, but truly one of his most imperial gifts was as a maker of Irish stew. 'The man who put the stew . . .' I don't know on what day of the week this stew was first made, but it likely served him for the duration. Like his clothes, his diet was unvarying and simple and well proved. I am not saying that this was the greatest stew ever made, as regards cuisine, as such. But you see, it was Donal's stew. It was the thing he had fashioned with his own hands. It was a magician's victual. Just lamb (or mutton maybe), potatoes and carrots. If there was seasoning in it, it was just salt and pepper. It was exactly the same stew my great-aunt Annie (now played by Tina) had made for us as children in the tiny cottage in Kelshabeg (now an important locus in this very play in rehearsal) except Donal's sported more meat – Annie only could afford a few lumps of mutton at the bottom of the pot, for the man who was working, say, but not for children. We had got only the essence, the aroma, the floating fat of the lamb, as children eating from the pot – like a very metaphor for a writer's memory.

This was Donal, the great bird of Donal, and he had slipped me under his wing, for all sorts of unfathomable reasons.

The day came when Donal felt obliged to shave his splendid hair as a preparation to play Thomas Dunne –

who was after all in his seventies and not likely to sport that dense helmet.

He was at a particular point in his meticulous exhumation of Thomas Dunne – retrieving a lost man from the Devil's Acre of Irish history, as it were. The character as I said was based on a great-grandfather who had served in the Dublin Metropolitan Police before independence. A troubling ancestor, shrouded in unwelcome history. He had been among the officers notoriously arresting James Larkin in Sackville Street, in a worrying photograph of the time. Even his descendants didn't know where exactly he was buried. Both his family and history had quietly ditched him, it seemed. Years after the show, my beloved friend Dermot Bolger helped me find him, using the new search technology in Glasnevin. He had been lying there all along, in an unmarked grave, just a few bones no doubt under a dusty nowhere, just hard by where Donal used to live. By then I wasn't able to tell Donal about it, but it would have given him a somewhat medieval satisfaction.

His job as he saw it was not to have an opinion about Thomas in any shape or form, but to become him. To become him without grace or favour, without regret or condemnation or judgement, even though in his personal politics Donal's identification was entirely with the working person, the so-called common man and woman, and the radiant citizen, and indeed the workless person – on his way to rehearsals he never passed the man begging on Hungerford Bridge without giving him a fiver, a tenner.

To become Thomas. This process he achieved, I realised perhaps also only years later, with the most patient, inching, unhurried, radical confidence not only in what he was doing, but in what the aether around him was doing, conspiring with himself and Max and all the other actors and officers of the play – we had been shown the most gorgeous designs and lighting plans – to bring what might be seen as an essentially artificial object, a play, to essentially otherworld and magical life. It was an incremental assault, almost imperceptible, like the slow coming of new fresh weather across a winter-benighted landscape. So much so that, coming into our last week of rehearsal, now rehearsing in the theatre itself, when the new artistic director of the Court came to see a ragged run-through, he told Max that while he thought it was fine, he saw no Big Performance there. Max, with the grim satisfaction of the experienced boxer, told me this, grimly. So then I merely hoped we might survive the three weeks in the sixty-seater theatre without too much shame. My fear as you can imagine was that the play would not be good enough ultimately for Donal, and that it would let him down. Then your only hope is to get out of Dodge without too many fatal bullets lodged in your backside. At that moment it seemed that might be the best ambition.

But Max worked on meticulously, marking his own script with his tiny writing. He was so impressive in his Russian doggedness. Certainly Max and Donal had forensically entered into every sentence of the play. Very little had been changed, but the little changes were like a vaccine to the fever of an unknown text. I suppose in truth Max had secretly 'actioned' the text – or shall we say, with high diplomacy. Max had an utter respect for Donal and he believed that Donal was the greatest actor he had ever worked with. Nevertheless even the lamb of God needs a shepherd. Just as Donal had let the script both talk to him and yet lie low, his performance at this point was lying low. If Max was concerned, he said nothing. On they worked, syllable by syllable. It's worth noting that the one actor in the company who perhaps hadn't been convinced about the play looked – at the very same showing that hadn't quite impressed the artistic director, at least in Max's sobering telling – very pale afterwards and was overwhelmed by Donal. 'That's my grandfather,' she said, weeping. 'Oh, I see what I'm in now.' And yet it was probably best, on balance, to hope for the best and prepare for the worst, as they say. This is why theatre is so difficult and challenging, and requires lorry-loads of mensch-like courage, which I have sometimes found I must admit only in thimblefuls in myself.

Meanwhile, in the interests of stew and ongoing nourishment, Donal brought his shaved head into his local shop and hoiked a bag of potatoes onto the counter. The shopkeeper contemplated the shaved head, the unshaven cheeks, the awful leather jacket, the crumpled clothes, and, making a monetary calculation, a humanitarian gesture, a gesture of social charity, said he could sell the potatoes singly to Donal if he needed. Perhaps another soul might have been offended – Donal took it as a fierce authentication of his new self as Thomas.

In the rehearsal room Donal was now finding dozens of vivid moments everywhere in his performance. Many things I witnessed and was delighted by, only for the gesture or the inflection, the whole discovery, to have been discarded overnight and replaced with a new wonder. Or rigorously pruned away. I wanted to beg him to keep certain things but I had learned long ago not to second-thought an actor.

And of course, those poisonous nerves developing to an intolerable pitch as we neared our opening night.

Previews didn't calm the nerves much. I am sure on the phone home to Ali I was gloomy enough. Probably not welcome news to a person juggling two two-year-olds dawn to dusk, her bloody absent partner seemingly coming a cropper in London. Pennilessness, McDonald's, rocky previews, O my Heavenly Jesus. Brian Friel came in and our mutual agent told me he had 'some reservations'. Hmmm. My lovely friend Billy Roche, at that time the most important new voice in Irish theatre on the London stage, seemed to hold my arm a little pityingly in the pub afterwards. I sensed his sympathy and his fear for me. I thought, here we go, over the waterfall into the abyss. I was wondering was there a shop in theatreland that would sell the appropriate life jacket. Would anyone mind if I suddenly emigrated to a country without English-language newspapers?

But something else was happening. The old BBC arts programme *Kaleidoscope* came in to the third preview, and issued an injunction to London to 'Hurry, hurry to *The Steward of Christendom*!' On the day we opened, the AD went down to get the *Evening Standard*, and the vendor said, handing it over with a very early review of the play in it, 'I think you'll be alright with this one, guv.'

As I am constitutionally unable to sit in with an audience at one of my plays, I was somewhat in the dark as to what had occasioned this enthusiasm. Maybe it was just an anomalous flare-up before the deluge came down on our heads? But something else, something strange, something that was the answer to the slow, deliberate questioning that Donal had made of the play – who are you, what are you, how do I become you, sit in you, make you sing and cry, bit by bit – was happening. Maybe 'happening' was the right word, in a John Lennon sort of way.

'This is not a play,' declared Donal. 'I know what it is. It's a performance piece.'

For him, I could intuit, it was certainly not a play – it was a conduit, or a system of complicated many-coloured wiring, back into the past, and deep into his own bright-dark self. His purpose was somehow by doing this play to resolve the great unresolvable thicket, the muddled wool basket of self, at the very heart of him. The distressing matters that had no doubt led him to drink so fiercely, consummately even, and that now in his oddly sainted sobriety were there even more fiercely to be rawly contemplated, understood, included, and by this means withheld, stopped from killing him. For Donal, as his friend Stephen Rea once said to me, doing a play was Life and Death. He didn't perform in your play, he used his selected text as a slippery manual of retrieval and ultimate survival. Like the awful instructions for some impossible homemade rocket. He placed himself in this veritably toxic nuclear stew of memory and reference, thereby by miraculous courage to remake himself, and in doing so, bizarrely almost, but certainly wonderfully, bring back from the cold hand of ordinary death a character both unmissed, with no known grave, but also, in being shown in all his ambiguity and contradiction by this alchemy of Donal, suddenly, in theatre form, understood, humanly *seen*, *loved* by the audience.

And as a consequence, all our efforts, the effort to write the play after the wonderful catastrophe of the twins, and Max's effort to marshal everything like a stoic general, and the inspirations and flashes of genius of Tina, and Kieran, and the rest, were suddenly rewarded by a cascade of praise and joyous welcome and extravagant high talk. Make no mistake, it was because of Donal. But he included us in his triumph, he implicated us in it. And it was an astonishing moment to reach. At that moment they could have given him the Nobel Prize for almost any division – Physics, Chemistry, Medicine, Literature.

We came to the Gate Theatre – an Irish play funded by the British Council to tour in Ireland, such was the grace and hope of the approaching peace in Northern Ireland – we toured the Antipodes, we had a second season in Dublin, and then went to New York.

———

We had many adventures with the play, which we never got tired of relating and repeating to ourselves. The night President Mary Robinson came to see it at the Gate. She was scheduled to come backstage afterwards to talk to Donal. Many minutes went by. He was in his tatty dressing gown, and he hadn't had a chance to take off his make-up and have a wash, and now here he was being delayed. He was sitting in the actor's steam of 'afterwards', an ember of the great fire of the performance that needed something poured on it, if not now alcohol, at least his famous Britvic and water, pint glass. Where in the name of Jaysus was she? Donal's patience, which could be infinite, was often preceded by an immense brewing impatience – in this he was bewilderingly back to front. You could be happy to be out of his way in those moments.

But the president was worth waiting for, surely, and he admired her, he was willing to sit there, waiting, waiting – up to a point. At last the front of house man, heroically immune to the moods of great actors, brought her in. She was so sorry, but she had been deeply moved by the play. She explained that she had needed a good ten minutes in the loo to straighten her mascara. Donal darkly sitting there, *glaring* benignly – immensely pleased.

Another night, Donal, even in the total concentration of carrying such a part as the Steward ('Even Lear gets to take a piss,' he pointed out to me), yes, even as he navigated the long speeches and the beautiful lighting changes, and the whole Raleigh-like voyage to other worlds and times, and wrestled with his daughters, and missed his daughter Dolly, and spoke of eggs and cows and uniforms and loyalties and finally the dog who was let live, nevertheless noticed that at the centre of the auditorium there was an empty seat. We were a sold-out show and it really vexed him to see this, one empty seat in a ten-week run. He was actually outraged. The same Ulyssean front of house man was summonsed to his dressing room afterwards. He was obliged to breast this barely controlled fury of an esteemed actor. 'I'm really sorry, Donal, we had a busload of pensioners coming up from the midlands. I'm afraid there was a problem with one of them at the last minute that resulted in the empty seat. I am truly sorry.'

'What problem, what problem?' said Donal, committed to his annoyance, and if he had been obliged to supply a verb in actioning, it would have been 'wounds'. He was on the cusp of even greater fury. Probably a fury that would melt the Arctic ice cap.

'The gentleman in question I am afraid . . .'

'Yes?'

'Well . . .'

'Yes?!'

'Died, Donal, he died.' Just for a moment it seemed the fury might blaze up anyway. Donal considered this for a burning moment. Was it really an adequate excuse? Mere death? An empty seat! Alright, alright, maybe it was.

'Alright,' he said. 'My condolences to the family.'

'I'll be sure and pass them on,' said the hero.

I wasn't there, but that might have been the gist of it.

He was as alert to historical moments as he was to empty seats. The play had premiered between the IRA ceasefires of the mid-nineties. Donal was deeply concerned not to claim any political significance for the play, which he thought would be most insensitive and offensive.

'We'll say nothing about that,' he said to me, sternly. I took my orders.

A year later the play as I say transferred to the Brooklyn Academy and *Newsweek* duly called Donal one of the Greatest Living Actors. And so he was. Great and Living and immense. And I still long, even after twenty years, for him to be so living, still in life, full of life, in gold light, still there mid-stage right, growling *Hurry up*, eternally.

Before that happened he had been down in Australia touring the play. Max and Sonia had been offered a fifteen-week run on Broadway but Donal rang me from Sydney to say he couldn't face that, and would I please understand. It would be eight shows a week and he didn't think he could survive that.

'I'm tired,' he said, 'at the very heart of me.' It was an accurate and innocent diagnosis of the very trouble that was brewing in him, and that would only become evident a year later, an illness at the heart of him that hurried him out of life. Somebody, in trying to get him to agree to Broadway, had pointed out to him that Jessica Tandy, then in her eighties, was doing a show on Broadway, which involved *dancing*. I'm not sure I can repeat what he said to that, but it was blunt. I absolutely understood, but I was relieved when he later agreed to the shorter run at BAM, just from a selfish, nappies-and-baby-food point of view.

Donal was delighted that the play had made money for us and he exulted eventually in coming to our new house in Greystones, and having his dinner with us – spuds and smoked mackerel being his elected menu. He truly, visibly exulted. He knew he had effected something life-changing and signal for us, and it seemed to give him the deepest satisfaction. He always said wondrous things about the play in interviews, though he did them rarely. In interview mode he was like a hermit asked to leave the Skellig of the actual production and come to the mainland to talk about it. But it was not really about the play, or the performance even, or your place in the theatre, or the this and that of prizes and aftermath, for me. It was really about having that man at one end of the story coming down into our flat, and then at the other end of the story sitting at the table in our new house, which he had willy-nilly provided, while he ate his mackerel with the untoward relish of the just.

I seemed to be with him a lot and felt very bound to him, laced into him, connected now by strange cables. I was somewhat aware of the dark misdemeanours of his drinking days, but it was hard not to revere and love him, and sober indeed he did seem to have a sort of saintly atmosphere around him. Saintly is not quite the right word perhaps. But it was as if he was being written now by Homer rather than O'Casey. Perhaps that is even less precise. But I felt there was something properly inexplicable about him, something immense and beyond the human, like those brooding landscapes described in Conrad's fiction. Even his courtesy, the courtesy of a man only too capable of utterly crushing remarks, was formidable. I would shake my head at the mystery of Donal, often and often.

All throughout this hour of talking to you I have laboured to present him to you, to remind you of him, to place him here again, all present and correct. Some of you will have known him better than I did, and worked with him longer. I haven't said enough about his photography, his drawing, his love of the horses, a thousand things, and much to my surprise I have confined myself to talking of life, and spurned other searing memories of his last days. My first title was actually 'Death of an Actor'.

But life, it was life he wanted, in the upshot. He lives permanently in his roles on film, especially Bob Quinn's and most especially as Gabriel Conroy in John Huston's film of Joyce's 'The Dead'. But his ineluctable greatness on stage is inevitably being lost, as the two hundred performances of a play are obliged to fade. People attest that they will never forget him in *Faith Healer*, in O'Casey's *Juno*, but nonetheless they cannot bequeath their memories. We can only write them down in a shadowy record of once highly charged corporeal things. Donal himself felt part of the honour of the theatre was that it is such a ruthlessly temporal affair. Being only of the moment, and paradoxically its eternity consisting of that. An empty theatre in the darkness content to host its silent shadows. Not to be tainted with pretending otherwise perhaps. He refused to film *The Steward* in any shape or form, and was determined, in almost a religious way, that his work would be seen, but then gradually be unseen, seen backwards, receding, erased, removed.

———

I suppose there are mysteries and alchemies in the theatre we hesitate to give credence to, as being fanciful. But at the end of the play on the few nights I saw it, it was quite clear to me he was no longer Donal, as such. Whoever he was, stirring there in the dying light, having told his last story to his son on the bed, and finally his son turning towards him and letting his smaller arm fall across his father, both of them rescued into sleep, or something deeper, it wasn't really Donal. Even the face looked different, darker, other. I suppose he had simply become Thomas. His favourite time in the play was just after that, when the audience would make not a sound, sometimes for minutes, no sound, no sound. Then slowly, as if coming back themselves into the shocking present, as if awakening from the dream of Donal's making, risking a few tentative claps, as if maybe they feared they were not in a theatre after all, but in some other realm of human truth and tattered majesty, where making the usual noises of approbation, the gathering applause and cheering, might be a violation.

This was all Donal's work, ultimately, and that was accepted by all. On his final performance in the play, at BAM in New York, having steadfastly refused previously ever to step forward from the line of actors at the curtain call, in old Abbey Theatre style, on this one night he did. And not only stepped forward, but stepped *down* into the auditorium, where the audience parted like running mercury, like a tiny Red Sea. And he walked forward to stand at the centre of them, not changing his expression, glaring, as serious as Sophocles, not acknowledging them quite, but radiantly present with them, transmuting in those moments from the beautiful relict of an ancient man that he had played for two hours, that Thomas, into this democratic colossus, this actor of actors, this Donal. And the audience instinctively acknowledged him with an unrestrained crescendo of applause, not only for his performance, but for this overwhelming manifestation of his mysterious self, and the primacy of theatre as the unrepentant enemy of time. And it was like the most beautiful and just full stop ever marked on a manuscript. A wordless summing up and an immutable final word.

And that was the last performance he ever gave in a theatre, eternally:

'And I would call that the mercy of fathers, when the love that lies in them deeply like the glittering face of a well is betrayed by an emergency, and the child sees at last that he is loved, loved and needed and not to be lived without, and greatly.'[1]

---

[1] These are the last spoken lines of *The Steward of Christendom*.

The Fog of Family

Third Laureate Lecture

Delivered online
International Literature Festival Dublin
30 May 2021

Here is a first memory, or masquerading as one.

It is of the bars of a cot, but not my own cot. It is in the old room of a hospital. I know where this hospital is – a Georgian building that still exists on Harcourt Street in Dublin. I remember tall windows and gloom and also that signature foggy bareness of childhood recollections. It may have been full of nameless medical clutter all the same.

Indistinct, the fog blowing through everything.

I am possibly one and a half years old. I must be walking, in order for my sister to be able to push me down the front steps of our house, as she has innocently done, causing me to break my nose. Then it duly healed and then she pushed me out a window. But it was the ground floor and it merely served to break my nose again.

My sister was not a murderer, she was a child consumed by a powerful emotion. For a year and a half, she had been the only child. Then, the interloper arrived.

The outcome was I began to speak through my nose, in so far as I was speaking. A surgeon attempted to rectify it. Hence the hospital cot. I am staring at the door into the ward, willing my mother to come back to me. I have no idea how long I have been waiting. Minutes or hours or days. I am standing on the mattress and holding onto the bars and I am staring at the solid-looking dark space. The need in me for my mother to come is absolute. The door must be already open, but so positioned that a person entering will only be seen at the last moment in the frame. My eyes are so focused the air is shifting and blurred as if with the smoke of a fire. In this memory my mother never comes. I am willing her to appear. Staring and staring. She never comes, she never comes.

And then she did.

———

The surgeon was working to clear the passageways of the nose, and he did, but inside things were still shattered, out of place. The most signal consequence of this deviated septum is I have been snoring like a walrus all my life. I knew nothing of that snoring version of myself till recently. Alas there is an app for everything. Listening to a recording of what the app designates as 'epic' snoring was not very Virgilian or Homeric.

The person who lies at my side has had thirty-five years of it. How can you apologise for thirty-five years of concatenation? A voucher for Brown Thomas doesn't cut that mustard.

I did not know the snorer in myself, the snoring husband, just as I am sure I do not really know the writer in myself. Or the child. That fictional, story-bound child.

But maybe all you need is a vague sense of yourself.

When I was a child and older, my father's snoring echoed through our old house on Longford Terrace, making, it seemed, the four-foot-thick walls tremble. We feared to wake that slumbering colossus. We used to creep up the stairs to bed, the heavy mahogany treads creaking. I have it all joined in my mind with Bach's cello suites, one of two records he owned, which also used to reverberate through the house, when it was being played on the gramophone. It was Pablo Casals as an old man, sawing 'his wife' in two, eternally, with many an audible groan. I suspect *he* snored to beat the band.

All in all, despite the snoring (my father's, not mine), I was having a happy childhood. A person can attempt to make an assessment of that, right or wrong, as he or she exits that demanding state of being. I loved my father. Even when I was a teenager, I relished his company in the mornings on the way into town to school, in the Volkswagen hatchback, one of a dynastic series of such cars since infancy. I missed his company even as I enjoyed it.

By the time I was in my early thirties, various family troubles had separated us permanently.

I remember the first sand-coloured Volks arriving, second-hand, cheap maybe but still coveted, pulling up to the pavement outside our flat on Leeson Park. Where indeed my sister did the work on my nose. Through a sunlight so piercing it was as good as a fog. Was I three? It must be a memory later than the hospital so. An even earlier memory than both of these was me smearing the contents of my nappy on the wall behind my cot, to the distress of my sister, who shared the room – maybe she had a motive for murder after all – but which my mother interpreted as an early sign of artistic ability. Indeed my grandfather, my father's father, who was a watercolourist of radiant ability, apprenticed me to him when I was about eleven. He hoped by doing so that I would continue on from him. Every Saturday I traipsed over to him after school. He always slept for an hour after lunch, so I would sit in his studio, waiting for him, waiting for his tread on the stairs, and the beginning of the miracle of watching him paint – his hands like miniature ballet dancers. A deep silence in the house. Like a spaceship in space. The studio as composed as a painting, with me, aged twelve, painted into it.

Snoring, an activity we share, my father and I. The only one now, separated as we have been for many years.

Did my grandfather, Papa Barry, his father, snore? I have no one to ask. I was only in his bedroom the once, and he was awake, if on the very cusp of his eternal sleep.

In all that there was a serious mystery. My grand-father had fallen out with his own father in Cork in some way. Was it because some of his half-brothers donned a British uniform and fought in the First World War? Or one of the full brothers? This great-grandfather, Patrick Barry, had two wives (not at the same time). There's a couple of brothers there I see, in the census for 1911, older than him. One is a train engine degreaser, the other a lithographer. Maybe they went to fight. A train engine degreaser sounds like a useful person in a war. It must have been complicated, because in the Cork records, there's Patrick Barry joining the Cork Brigade of the IRA in summer 1914, as the Great War actually broke out. He was sixty-four, quite old for a revolutionary. The 1916 rising in Cork city was called off by Eoin MacNeill. Nevertheless, numbers in Cork managed to become besieged in the City Hall by British soldiers (some of them native Irishmen of course) and held out for a week. I don't know if my grandfather and his father even were among them, I like to think they were. Except in another record I see my grandfather was training in Dublin at the time as an art teacher (aged twenty-three). Father and son together, before the break. Or father and son sundered, in some way unknown. Just like myself and my father.

What was the trouble that parted them? I do wonder. Was it because he married Maud Dunne, the daughter of a superintendent in the Dublin Metropolitan Police? He never said and I don't know. Curiously enough, despite being a Corkman, my grandfather was a fervent follower of de Valera (who was from Clare via New York, whereas Michael Collins was a real Corkman) so I have to suppose he opposed the Treaty of 1922 brokered by Collins in London, and was on the irregular side in the Civil War to boot, but again, I don't know, because he never said, or I never asked. But that might have caused a rift too.

Fogginess abounding, abundant.

The fog of family. It swirls about, it's very thick in

places. Glimpses only are granted, that prompt novels certainly.

My grandfather won an imperial scholarship, ironically, to study painting at Goldsmiths' in London, probably around the time that Michael Collins was working in the post office there. Were they both stirred by the news from home, in their different London lairs? Did they know each other? Dislike each other?

I would like to ask the ghost of Kitty Kiernan, a friend of other ancestors, on my mother's side, the Sheridans of Omard, if Collins snored. But maybe better to ask Lady Lavery? Everyone loved Collins, even the people that assassinated him – maybe they most of all. He was only a young man, handsome as Valentino. When his fiancée Kitty Kiernan, her parents at that time already dead, was burned out of her hotel in Granard during the War of Independence, she was rescued by old Maria Sheridan, my grandmother's aunt, up there in Omard, County Cavan. It was the IRA burned Kitty out, in reprisal for her allowing a young Dublin RIC policeman to drink in her hotel bar. Collins was horrified, he was on the same side of course as the arsonists, but hadn't known about the reprisal – which is interesting in itself. Many of the rural commands were not linked to Dublin directly, for security maybe. Anyway, the Sheridans of Omard were well-to-do Catholic landowners, strong farmers, and Kitty found refuge there in the old house that now stands in ruins, an unlucky building. They favoured priests, bank managers and the Catholic middle classes in general, and had fishing parties in May when the may-fly were up, and tennis parties, all of which seems very surprising – you would have got a telegram from Maria saying just that, if you were a favoured guest – *Mayfly up*. The Catholic landed class and all its accoutrements and favoured activities, entirely vanished away. And Collins himself visited her there, and played tennis on the court, under the great trees, and no doubt ate heartily at Maria's groaning country table. I never knew my grandmother, Mai Kirwan, whose mother, like Maria's mother, had been one of the Galligan legatees, five girls who had been given dowries by a relative who had grown rich in Argentina but was childless. And the girls married into rich farms in Cavan, and brought their South American dowries with them, gold coins in bags, except Mai's mother, who married an insurance broker with a nice house in Galway. And then my grandfather, who mar-ried Mai, managed to bet away that house on the horses, and indeed the bag of gold coins too, all unbeknownst to

Mai, ah, poor Mai, poor Mai – but I have tried to write about all that in *The Temporary Gentleman*.

Oh my heavens, continuing rolling masses of fog, masses. And where does it all leave me?

This grandfather, Jack O'Hara, who married Mai: I shared a bed with this duly widowed man (Mai died in 1953 of liver cancer and alcoholism) in the deep cold of those Irish winters – the foghorn like a sounding whale out in the wild dark around Monkstown Pier – and in summer had my own bed in the same room, so I think I can state categorically he never snored, though to be honest he was inclined to stay awake deep into the small hours, when I heard him rustling the racing paper as a defence against dreams. Real fog and family fog, all swirling about. He'd read the form on horses all hours of the night – and then tragically back the favourites anyway. Which was never profitable. Maybe he did snore, when I was too sunk in sleep to know.

He told me everything about his life except the (myriad) bad things, which is fair enough. That was his highly effective smokescreen, and would have worked even better if my mother had not specialised, usually in another part of the flat, in telling me all his secrets anyway, in vivid detail. He disliked my father intensely, which puzzled and confounded me. Fiercely, in that familial whisper. We all lived in the same few rooms. There was a lot of fierce whispering.

I am old enough to call them my people, that old tribe I was born into. Stories on top of stories, built on top, memories on memories, like the ancient conquered cities in the Bible. And everywhere, that fog creeping. Which sometimes seems to complicate everything, to queer every pitch and stop every clock.

Some of those fog-bound stories seem to loom nearer than the present, with its pristine visions. And even if I know the shortcomings of all these people, the whole crew of them, I am old enough to know my own too, and I am honour-bound to judge them in the round. Which is also very complicating. But whatever and whoever they really were, I will have become a writer as a consequence of them. Even if I didn't know them properly, with clinical forensic eyes, even if I don't know them now, they will still have made me a writer.

Not asking is a feature of much lost history, we may suppose. Time itself asks no questions, it marches bluntly, mutely, on. Perhaps it has no questions, or none worth asking, or none anyone or anything would know the answers to. In the case of my painter grandfather, and his revolutionary exploits, I was too young to ask really, being a very naïve and peculiar young man when that grandfather died in 1974, not political myself and not very aware of such things, or even interested, despite being in my second year at Trinity College. Or because of that. The confusions of youth that felt like certainties, clarities. I had no idea it would be my life's work to dig into those secrets, those things unknown, half seen. To peer through the fog for forty-five years. In 1974 it had been some years since I had seen my grandfather, whom I loved so much when I was a boy, because at college I had grown my hair not just below the collar, but right down to my waist, and although I thought this was the proper look for the early seventies, he didn't. When he was said to be dying, I went to his house on Morehampton Terrace (in those days modest lower-middle-class dwellings), stuffing my hair down into my shirt at the back so it would be hidden, and was let in by his second wife Anna, once a nurse at Guinness's brewery, a very kind, soft woman from Cavan, who was always anxious about the regularity of what she called 'movements', *have you had a movement today?* – and walked right through the inner spaces of childhood most valuable to me, the full-remembered house, starting with the big Bakelite bell at the front door, the hall with its rack of coats and its fancy barometer (at which he used duly to glance going out, even though the actual weather lay inches away), the self-painted panels of the doors of his best room (with the sacred black porcelain sweet jar), the hubcap of a car on the wall in the gloom of the back corridor beyond, that he had hung there in playful homage to the famous Van Eyck painting, the stairs with its sequence of stormy views of the Poolbeg lighthouse and the Great South Wall, and further up, photographs of my father and my uncle as beautiful young men. Then the soapy smell from his bathroom, whose unsilvering mirror he had rescued with little flowers in oil paint, the plug on the bath a substantial machine of someone's strange invention, and on into the back bedroom, with its surprising double bed (I had never been in there before, I realised), its hedgy and apple-tree privacy, and my grandfather there, in his last days or hours, his face blank initially, then suddenly smiling, suddenly knowing me, beyond caring about long hair maybe, full of love – the powers vanishing out of his veins, out of everything, deserting his cherished self – but this victorious moment at least left balancing in the aftermath, left resonating, left a permanent boon really, his precious smile of pleasure. Clear as sunlight.

My father used to tell a story, that when Papa Barry's father was dying, he *did* go back down to Cork. My great-grandfather, who was poor all his life, and worked as a fuller in a carpet factory, gave his son as his inheritance a pair of working boots, which were under the bed in a paper bag. 'Only a little used,' he said.

Two years later when I left Trinity, I had my contentious hair cut off and I sold it to a wig-maker in Dunleary, who said it was high-quality stuff even suitable for a woman's wig and it would last forever. Somewhere in the world my hair is still walking around.

In life Papa Barry had looked after his two pairs of leather shoes – very nice shoes, not boots – with such precision and care that they not only lasted him a lifetime, as he had once prophesied, but outlived him. When my sister and I went to fetch the paintings he had left us after his death, there they were, the two pairs of shining shoes, outside his bedroom door, patiently waiting for him to come back out. When I looked closely at them, they were a little scumbled and old, but when I stood back from them, yes, they were perfect – the exact principle of art he had taught me as a child. The painter works close in, but what he is doing should be seen from six feet away. That's why he was always walking away from his easel,

walking away, and walking back, with his serious face, his
painting hand as sure and steady as metal, and if not, then
he had a stick to steady it against the sized cardboard or
the drawing paper. And faraway mountains in a picture,
the ones furthest away, were always blue. I was to remember that. The sky might be every colour, it might well
be blue in part, but the mountains furthest away were
always blue. He wore a brushed trilby which he lifted to
ladies coming out of shops in adjacent Donnybrook, and
wanted the whole country to be speaking Irish as the efforts of his generation deserved. He taught drawing to
ungrateful pupils in the Technical College in Ringsend.
He paid rent all his life and even when my father offered
to buy his house for him, he didn't want the bother of it.
In the summer he wore a neat straw hat in the garden.
He made an Australian bullroarer for me because he had
seen it described in a book. He was to me a poem somehow intimately bound up with his apple tree that only
gave apples every second year, his roses, his nasturtiums
that he grew to conceal a little midden, and the spiders
in the back wall that was high because it bordered on a
sombre monastery. Here he and I stood betimes, while
he gently tipped the webs with a stick, so that the huge
spiders would come out to thrill us, thinking we were

flies. He was a small man in stature, with something of a pot belly, bravely shown in a lovely self-portrait in charcoal of himself at his easel – now hanging in my own sitting room. With his first wife Maud a shadowy drawing on the wall behind him. A drawing of a drawing.

I don't know where it leaves me, but these memories are certainly a comfort.

Did he have to kill, during the Rising, during the Civil War?

With all the universe-wide passion of a child, I loved him.

It strikes me that it was maybe *not* asking pertinent things that helped make me a writer. You ask and answer yourself later, in the presence of these ghosts.

As a creature of the fog.

My other grandfather, the one I shared the bed with, my mother's father, whom we called Mair Papa as a childish version of Mary's Papa – Mary being my mother's sister, a famous singer and harpist in her day – was altogether a different kettle of Irish fish. His father, Old Pat, had been leader of a dance band in Sligo, Pat O'Hara's Orchestra, that served the dancehalls thereabouts, but he was also a tailor in the Sligo Lunatic Asylum. Both this great-grandfather and my grandfather were painfully aware of some real or imagined fall in social stature, and my grandfather laboured to put this right, serving first, a boy of sixteen, as a radio operator in the British merchant navy in the last few months of the First World War, then taking up work as an engineering officer in the British Foreign Service, building bridges across Africa and, I suppose, burning his own. In the Second World War he rose to major in the Royal Engineers, mostly in the dangerous task of bomb disposal. All these occupations returned to him a sense of social position, but also, of course, alienated him effectively from the main current of Irish experience after independence. To my other grandfather he would have had all the edgy glamour of a traitor.

A brave man though, defusing those bombs. He said he used to sit on the bombs when he was drawing out the fuse, as it fell to the officer to do, so that if it went up he would be killed immediately, and not left maimed.

Well, I loved them both, these epical grandfathers, though they generated more fog between them than an Irish coast, and I remember an odd moment, when the Sligo grandfather (always scandalous, as he had been a terrible and destructive drinker, though now sober) had come to fetch me from visiting the revolutionary grandfather (never touched a drop in his life), and I looked back out through the reverse-slanting rear window of the Ford Anglia and saw these two men, at the little iron gate, talking briefly, unusually, and, for a short shining moment in the lost sunlight of an Irish day, shaking hands with sudden cordiality, which pleased me obscurely.

These two men – both my grandmothers died young and I never knew them – were in their different ways what you might term 'positively charged'. Though there was a touch of something eating away at them both, and though both had their oddnesses and their troubles, even so they seem to me to have been on the side of life, and fully living, and expressing somehow wordlessly a humble gratitude arising from that.

———

I think it is fair and sad to say that my father was negatively charged, at least for me – and even my mother, though she had all the appearance and behaviour of a live wire, or a cut wire thrashing about after a storm, having been torn from its proper place. My mother was therefore as perilous ultimately as you might expect such a ruptured thing to be. But she was also vivid and highly present, which as a child I found an enchantment. His more or less Sartrean nihilism and her – can I respectfully call it – hecticality generated a lot of fog, certainly. This isn't to say I didn't love them. When I was a child I was their small ambassador, and praised them, as it were, to strangers, foe and friend alike. I thought at least I *knew* them with that forensic instinct of a child that allows us to suspect that all our proper research is done from age two to ten. But if I knew certain aspects of them, the ones visible to me, of which I entirely approved, the ten-year-old more than willing to give them the palm of emperor and empress, the fact is I didn't know them, I mistook them, and they didn't know themselves, to a tragic degree, and if they did, hid what they knew, from us, and just as tragically from themselves. Their narratives were menaced by a foggy disarray.

But it is better to be a child of a positively charged person, is my suspicion. Maybe, like the earthly poles, they switch about, sometimes positive, sometimes negative, or are different to different people. My mother was much loved in her profession. Like Donal McCann, if you had wired her up from that wild thrashing wire, you might have lit a city from her. But positive or negative, does it come to the same thing? What is known, what is not known, starts to merge into the one mystery, and has no helpful x and y. Dark matter, that we know is there only because there is no other explanation for what is visually missing.

———

The glories of my father. My father published a book of poems in the fifties with Dolmen Press, setting his own lines in type, as was the necessity of a nascent press. Thomas Kinsella was a fellow poet, John Montague later. The publisher of Dolmen, Liam Miller, turned down a young Seamus Heaney, the story goes – which apparently is both true and untrue, like most of human history. In 1969 my father, aged thirty-nine, published a thin volume called wonderfully *In Dante's Wood*, which Cyril Connolly, in almost his last act as a living person, praised very briefly in the *Observer*. My father's heroes were e. e. cummings, from whom he possessed a letter, an answer to a fan letter he had sent – all in lower case – and Joyce and Beckett, but not Synge or O'Casey, who were part of my mother's world in the theatre, which my father was not so comfortable with. He would go and see her

in plays but I am not sure he was ever at his ease doing
that. She would always show that other, powerful, public
side to her, the part of her that was so admired by other
actors, and I suspect her show of such great power un-
nerved him.

In the seventies, on our continuing journeys into
town, when I was by then attending Trinity College, he
would tell me about the novels he was writing. He felt he
had done something 'hitherto undone in Irish literature'.
But they were never published. I'm not sure why. I did
read one called *The Santorini Obsession*, which was ex-
tremely well written, but involved a lot of sex, which un-
nerved me, even aged twenty. I found my father all in all
a bit unnerving, as sons do sometimes. But I also found
him interesting, appealing, and thought him unusual and
impressive, and all in all credited to him at least a quarter of my 'happy childhood'. My mother being another
quarter of that in the main, with her penchant for fabulous outings to beaches round Dublin, her upblaze of
humour like the second thoughts of a forest fire. And I
loved the milieu where she worked, and all the forgotten
great actors of her time, whom I knew in Abbey Theatre
dressing rooms. Angela Newman, a Jewish genius
from Smithfield, who is still in my mind's eye in all her

lovingness and majesty. 'You will be so handsome when you grow up,' she said to me, aged six. Which was welcome news, even something of a relief. Donal McCann, who was himself very young, but not as young as me. Sinéad Cusack, as beautiful a person as you would ever see, and the both of them, Donal and Sinéad, beautiful, brilliant. I loved all that and I was privileged to be unofficially among them, after performances, in the dusty corridors and dressing rooms of the Queen's Theatre, where the Abbey held the line for the moment, after the famous fire, and while it awaited the rebuilding and opening of the so-called New Abbey, a brutalist monument, as it turned out, to the dainty old theatre, and with its huge stage and dire acoustics, the killer of many plays, some of my own among them.

Ah yes, Joan O'Hara, Siobhan Ní Eagra, in Irish – or Siobhan Niagara, as Donal called her. I often still miss her. I find myself suddenly, without warning, missing her. The fact of her. The shebang of her personality. Positive or negative charge sometimes doesn't come into it.

How quickly I slip up the decades in a mere few sentences. From my mother's work in the Abbey to my own. From my ten-year-old self put into the stalls by Lily Shanley, front of house manager, to my (to me alarming-looking – who is that distressed-looking person?) portrait hanging on the stairs that lead up to the glooms of the Abbey bar.

My mother was in rehearsal for the play that was to open just before that famous Abbey fire. In 1951 I think it was. She was twenty-one. We might have a moment of sadness for the playwright, since I don't think that play ever did open. But the fire burned a whole tradition, along with the old timbers and seats of a music-hall theatre that had once housed a morgue in its basement, and Dan Leno's famous clog dance on its stage. I think it was Padraic Colum the poet who said, going into the plush new modern Abbey, as it opened grandly, nationally, in 1966, 'The old theatre was good enough for me and Yeats.'

I don't know if any great Abbey plays date from the years of exile in the Queen's Theatre in Pearse Street, but the place was certainly stuffed with great actors, my mother among them. I remember Donal McCann telling me that his father, John McCann, almost single-handedly kept the theatre going with his succession of expert potboilers that always drew a crowd, as opposed to the different magics of Yeats or Lady Gregory. I like Frank O'Connor's story (or was it Seán Ó Faoláin's?

Or Padraic Colum's?) of going to see a Yeats play as a young man, and finding no one else in the theatre except one gentleman in the front row, gazing up, enraptured. A halo of white hair. Yeats himself. My mother worshipped Yeats and in particular his plays. When Coca-Cola funded a season of Yeats plays in the eighties, she was delighted, and quipped, 'Well, that's gas.' By another poetic confluence of Irish things, it was Donal McCann who continued the tradition of supporting carbonated drinks, when he did the once-famous voiceover for Ballygowan mineral water. 'Ballygowan – no other water.' He got the whole strange world of Ireland into four words. Donal, who died with the greatest reputation of any actor in the history of Ireland and not much more than a penny to his name. Who didn't even seem to notice he was in an antiquated public ward when he got ill. Or preferred it that way.

When Seamus Heaney would be in to see one of my plays, and I would be lurking nervously in the lightbox, his head of hair also would look like a halo, a planet, flaring and dying as the lighting design on stage dictated.

Like light through fog.

My father always had a problem with memory. When
he was a child, his head was run over by some sort of
light vehicle, maybe a bread van. Or maybe a delivery
boy's bicycle. Either way he spent a year in the Children's Hospital in Baggot Street, putting my own so-
journ in Harcourt Street hospital into the halfpenny
place. I hope he was visited regularly, but in truth his
mother by some accounts suffered from her nerves, and
was somewhat bedbound, so I don't know. After his
injury and his recovery, my uncle, his brother, said he
was never the same. Some sea-change had been effected
in him. Some sea fog had passed into his head. He was
highly functional at his studies and gained a scholarship
in architecture to Italy, above all the other contestants
of his year in Ireland. There used to be photographs of
him in his fifties garb, away there in Rome, Milan, Siena.
His raincoat, his neat beard, his John Lennon glasses
before John Lennon. He looked like Lytton Strachey or
a young French film star. But he was never the same,
apparently. What he had been like before I don't remember my uncle saying.

We were parted by family troubles, permanently, unfix-
ably. My grandfathers died, my parents separated, the
old house – the old theatre as it were – was sold. I met my
wife Ali in 1985, the twins were born in '92, and Toby
in '97. All the old maps and documents of family were
being superseded by this new family – one we were con-
structing ourselves. We weren't accidental invitees. Our
task was to protect it, to let our children feel the bounty
of safety, and that's what we did.

<hr />

A consequence of my sister's innocent attempts on my
life when we were little is I have no real sense of smell.
Or only a blurred and muted one. When in my work I
describe things, when it comes to smells I have to have
recourse to other texts, other evidence, other witnesses
with better noses. When a smell does reach me, I am
grateful. I am so grateful I am moved and stirred. A
particularly pungent rose. The sea served up to me at
Kilmichael Point in Wexford. My humanity seems fuller
for a moment. Perhaps a sense of smell is an essential part
of being human, of judging things, of knowing where you
are, your spiritual GPS.

Einstein of course tells us that we simply do not have the requisite senses to understand time. Its seeming narrative atmosphere, one thing following another, is provably not correct or even real.

So news from the past is always current. Nothing wants to be, or can be, history. This will be bad news for my beloved friend, Roy Foster, quondam Carroll Professor of Irish History at Oxford. But no, there is no such thing as the discrete past. All the riddle of my life, all the depth of my allotment of chaos, my share of happiness, finds its authorship in what used to seem the distant past and since it is not, ever, must always be wrestled with. The subtle duality of childhood is the angel we have been given to measure our strength against. To measure our work against.

My father and mother. This is a phrase that should engender a feeling of pride. The Bible tells us so. I have always been *inclined* to describe them as epic and memorable – a default position. In place of actually going to the trouble of knowing them, I invented them, sometimes right in front of their faces. But that is an old text. Who do we need as passionately as we do our parents? I remember reaching out a hand as a little child to touch my father's rich red beard. With his architect's board dominating the room and those first episodes of *Doctor Who*, in the person of William Hartnell – a victim of dementia even as he played the doctor – to scare us to death on the television. My father playing the *Doctor Who* theme tune on his silver whistle and myself reaching for his beard. Reaching out a small hand . . . Fascinated. We do it to love them properly. How *helplessly* I loved him. He was a man with many hidden things all his life, including his chin. Never seen since young manhood, as his father's photo of him on the stairs attested. His voice, his presence, his handsomeness, his personal gifts. His singing in falsetto on the way up past St John's church to school in Hampstead when I was six and my sister eight, *In spring time, in spring time, the only pretty ring time.* His unusual clothes, his filed fingernails, that trimmed russet beard. If the love of a child is your true and actual wealth, he was a millionaire. I know my sister felt the same. We worshipped him, we watched him, we waited for him, and we did not know him. We had gone to London so he could take up a post as an architect there, and my mother took those years off to look after us. I remember his curious friends, especially a man called Horise, who had been in a concentration camp as a little boy in, I think, Denmark. And I remember the sweet young lady who rented a room in our flat, and whose grand piano almost entirely filled it. All the painters, poets and mad persons of Hampstead in those days. Post-war – post many wars really, First World War, Irish War of Independence, Irish Civil War, Spanish Civil War, Second World War, the Shoah, the Cold War still icily rumbling. A fogbound coast of a generation. It is no wonder their hero was Sartre, that their bible was *Being and Nothingness*, and that maybe for them quite rightly, especially surely for Horise, family and history were dead, with atrocious literality, and love too into the bargain, in particular familial love. It is all very understandable and I may pity them but woe to you to be a child of such people.

Or perhaps not. The universe depends on everything being negatively and positively charged, that is the nature of its unity. Lucretius tells us so.

My mother. My instinct is still to speak well of her. I circle back and back. Brilliant, beautiful, powerful in her public life, way-giving, compliant, meek in her private. Funny, delightfully foul-mouthed, outrageously celebratory of being in the world, mushroom-gatherer, walk-goer, high-talker, perpetual crazy-girleen unicorn

– 112 –

of a mother. And yet, deaf to anything arising from the dark, oblivious. Her own mother and father, Mai Kirwan and her husband, Major John Charles O'Hara, destructive alcoholics which she had had to survive somehow. She did it by resolving never to know herself, never to see herself, never to ask questions to which the answers might be troubling. Who was born alone it seemed, lived alone within her own family, and definitively died alone, with no one at her bedside except a male nurse, myself, her son, far away in Greece on a family holiday, and indeed everyone else not there, absent, as her soul tried to fly out the window, like a panicking robin wandered into the house.

As I write this, I think, involuntarily, *my poor mother*. My strange, singular mother, an experiment in character from a single mould. Secretive, yes. Bipolar, according to her last doctor – hardly her fault. Whose playing of Lady Bracknell earned the extraordinary response from some long-gone Dublin critic, 'God will never forgive Joan O'Hara for her Lady Bracknell and nor will I.' How she delighted in that! 'Over the top? – yes,' she would say, 'over the top and into the bloody fray.' Who rose to the challenge of Lorca, Synge, Chekhov and her out-and-out favourite Yeats in a manner unique in the annals of Irish

theatre. Unconditionally admired by that same dismant-
ler of reputations, Donal McCann. A woman who went
as passionately to swim on White Rock beach in Dalkey
as she would sit like a fire on the first day of rehearsal of
a play. Who inspired, thrilled and amazed not just audiences but directors and fellow actors. Who in her last
years played the character of the curmudgeon Eunice
in the RTÉ soap opera *Fair City* with strange gusto. An
inveterate *worker*. When she was very ill and I found her
a nursing home in Kildare, she said, 'But, Bassy, that's
much too far away, I have to be in RTÉ at six a.m. every
morning.' A worker, stopped in her tracks. Did she care?
Wild uncaring was her way, mostly. But she cared about
that. Who put a pencil in my hand when I was two weeks
old and bid me write or draw.

We shouldn't go home to our parents, even metaphor-
ically, and give them any type of hell, because old hells
are neighbours to old heavens.

The child, nose broken or unbroken, knows nothing,
and yet he has seen everything. He has been a witness.
With his own eyes. Beside my bed in Hampstead I carved
out a hole in the plaster as if I was trying to get away. But
you can't get away when you are a child. You don't have
the legs for it and you don't know the train times.

The child sees only points of light, bravely takes his bearings from them, and knows nothing about all the dark matter around them.

The child is not the father of anything. His compass is just his foggy heart.

———

What are writers made of? Imponderable ocean-deep flotsam and wreckage. A jam jar of fog. A bell jar needed to glimpse anything. A shaken heart. A shocked face. A deviated septum. Out of these things we write, or try to write. And snore, snore to beat the band.

So maybe I must give thanks, finally. A difficult legacy is still a gift.

———

I have seen my father rarely in the last thirty years. In 2008 he caught me off guard on holiday with my wife and children on the island of Paros. We were just sitting down to lunch and he was there on the phone suddenly. Without thinking, longing to see him, I said I would come up to visit him in his house above Paroikia, the capital of the island. My eldest son Merlin, by then six-teen, said he would come with me.

You go up the wild mountain road and park at the old monastery and walk down the marble way. Adored country. Thyme scenting the path. I could smell that. Where was the mulberry tree, whose dark fruit the hedgehogs used to eat noisily in the Greek dark? Many years before I had spent the summer in the house with the builders. There was the piece of ancient marble set into the lintel of the door, that I had bought for two thousand drachmas and a bottle of whiskey. After all the years of my absence the house had reversed back towards decay, the dovecote edging towards ruin, the guest rooms empty and unpainted. When I had last seen it in 1983, it had had all the spank and glow of a finished restoration.

Nearly thirty years, I suddenly realised, had passed. Einstein, Einstein, come to my rescue, tell me again that time passing is an illusion.

As we came in the door he was sitting at the kitchen table and looking up his Greek dictionary and I asked him what word he sought. He said, the word for *traitor*. He said it quietly, calmly, his beautiful face composed. He was in a dispute with his neighbour over the question of a road and trying to compose a letter in Greek.

He needed to run the road across part of her land. She had agreed but now she was thinking twice. She wrote that she could not divide her late father's land, it was too painful. But my father needed the road, because at the moment there was a long walk from a neighbouring house, along a little path fretted with red butterflies and yellow broom, and his ankles were weak.

'Other than that,' he said, with justifiable satisfaction, 'there's nothing wrong with me.'

Traitor. Our very Irish word.

He was seventy-eight that year. I was fifty-three.

He took an instant liking to my son. He delighted in him. We talked about nothing, the most perilous topic of conversation. The grandfather gave the grandson an old panama hat as we were going, because he was worried about my son going around in the heat without a covering.

I thought, here is a coda to something, a precarious end. A moment with mercy in it, for everyone in the room.

———

I fear the fog I have tried to describe can never clear, except briefly. The door opens onto clear country, it closes again. And when the smoke does clear, it seems a desirable moment, but at the same time, a difficult one. Stark truths stand there monumentally in the cleared ground where you thought there was nothing, or not that, and I must admit one stares balefully at them sometimes. Regretfully. Could it all have been otherwise? We are talking about things that even clear vision can't unravel. Nothing *can* be done with the truth maybe. Or these old truths. My present family is such a different beast, there is clarity, simplicity, love. Fiction certainly wants ambiguity, things glinting and glimpsed, possible reversals and redemptions, deep fogs moving across erased landscapes, with their bursts of sudden sunlight, and its quick removal. Fiction likes the fog more than anything, it seems to me, out of which faces emerge, suddenly. Perhaps real truth comes through the battered eyes of fiction. The fog is ultimately beneficial, beneficent, acutely illuminating with its darknesses and erasures. It is the distillation, the subtle whiskey of truth.

And I have gone on writing only realising little by little that I know nothing about those lost figures, or the true meaning of any of the accidentals of their life. I write to balance the pendulum – more outrageously, to still it.

Perhaps to have known everything, in those early

years, to have seen everything, would have meant I could never be a writer.

As a child I was a connoisseur of happiness, when it struck. Only difficult sums, tricky calculus, can get you to the moon and back. There is an arena of experience mysteriously allotted us. The specifics are nearly irrelevant. What counts is your common sense of survival and your occasional exultation. It's what true sentences are made of. The fog doesn't matter as much as I thought, it is a pictorial addition. What remains is to still the pendulum, but also to recognise you are not the final agency of judgement. And when there is happiness in the consoling present, the ever-new present tense, even the writer, especially the writer, has a duty to notice, really to notice, to find yourself clear-eyed in its moment, but also rejoicing, untrammelled by self-consciousness or a cool maturity. So that the ashes and cinders of old things and memories can be transmuted into a strange currency, a trembling gold, with all the passionate fakery of the alchemist, all the redundant passion of the child.

ACKNOWLEDGEMENTS

My thanks to the Arts Council of Ireland for the great adventure of the laureateship, 2018–21. Also to the Gate Theatre for hosting two of the lectures. And to *Today with Sean O'Rourke* and *Today with Claire Byrne* for following the story of the laureateship on RTÉ radio. And to The Big O, and Arcade Films, for their work filming the lectures. And to my son Toby for recording the third lecture at home in Moyne. And to Cormac Kinsella, for his pristine PR work. And to Orlaith McBride and Kevin Rafter for introducing the lectures. And to Faber and Faber, and my editor Angus Cargill, for publishing them.